Balcony, Terrace and Patio Gardening

Margaret Davis

Cover design by Alyssa Pumphrey
Interior design by Jay Staten
Cover image copyright © 1997 Jerry Pavia

Library of Congress Cataloging-in-Publication Data

Davis, Margaret.
   Balcony, terrace and patio gardening / Margaret Davis.
      p.   cm.
   Originally published: Gladesville, Australia ; Golden Press Pty.
Ltd., 1981.
   Includes index.
   ISBN 1-55591-256-7 (pbk.)
   1. Balcony gardening. 2. Patio gardening. 3. Container gardening.
I. Title.
SB419.5.D38   1997
635.9'86—dc20
                              95-48079
                                CIP

Printed in Korea

0 9 8 7 6 5 4 3 2 1

Published in cooperation with the
International Center for Earth Concerns,
Conservation Endowment Fund

and

Fulcrum Publishing
350 Indiana Street, Suite 350
Golden, Colorado 80401-5093
(800) 992-2908 • (303) 277-1623

To the wonderful husband whose constant help

and encouragement made all my gardening

and writing possible.

Contents

Preface

I have been a balcony gardener for almost twenty years, since the time when acute arthritis forced me to reluctantly give up a large and much loved garden that my husband and I had created and tended over a period of thirty-one years, and also a smaller, but equally beloved, mountain garden where we grew all the marvelous cold-climate plants and trees.

There must be many aging couples like ourselves—dedicated gardeners who look back with sinking hearts to the scenes of former horticultural triumphs and defeats, feeling that an enchanting and never-to-be-repeated chapter of our lives has closed forever. And yet, how wrong we are! I am sure that there are just as many, if not more, younger people living in urban environments, remembering the lush gardens of their parents. They long for the beauty and peaceful retreats from their hectic lifestyles, yet have never gardened before.

Our balcony garden opened a whole new world of fascination and excitement with even more challenges than we met in our two large areas of land, and it gave us the novelty of learning to live in a quite different climate in a quite different country. The nostalgic backward glances ceased soon after we settled into our new apartment, and in their place came a delicious sense of freedom with the realization that we could now enjoy growing flowers with none of the time-consuming and backbreaking tasks of eternal pruning of overly exuberant branches, sweeping up fallen leaves, watering, watering, watering and worst of all, weeding, weeding, weeding!

True, the pests were still with us. How they managed to sniff out our treasures in what we thought was a safe hideaway fifteen floors above the ground will forever remain a mystery, and so again began the search for pesticides lethal to only the pests and not to the person wielding the spray. But challenges are the breath of life to gardeners, and how dull it would all be if everything just grew without any effort whatsoever on our part. But the battle with the pests is only one of those faced by the balcony gardener. Restriction of space can also mean a very difficult series of decisions and sad renunciation of plants that we would so much like to have grown. There is also the frustration of restrictions imposed by building codes that say "No" to the enclosing, or even partial enclosing, of windy open balconies that would provide needed protection for the delicate plants we all long to grow.

I even encountered a neighbor who stoutly maintained that she was allergic to plant life in any form, most especially perfumed flowers, and as she was allegedly slowly dying from the effects of my stephanotis and plumeria, I had to give in to a plea that these be summarily removed. Just when the buds that I had so longingly watched were opening! Even after this was done, I was assured that even the proximity of the foliage of all plants was untenable to this particular allergy, but fortunately other circumstances eventually caused the allergic one to depart, and then we were able to indulge in all the many fragrances that Hawaii's tropical climate provides in such abundance.

In fact, this ability to enjoy the many fragrances at close quarters is perhaps the greatest joy of balcony gardening. This, of course, applies to every climate, for while I had the tropical flowers only, the cold- and temperate-climate gardener can have a much greater variety. Think of the wallflowers, the stocks, petunias, the exquisite freesias and all the other spring bulbs and daphne! The list is long, and limited only by the enterprise and enthusiasm of the gardener; and it includes many vines. Vines to twine around doorways and windows, to give beauty as well as perfume and beautiful vines including the morning glory and the heavenly white moonflower—both flourish in a wide range of climates.

One of the interesting things about balcony gardening is that however experienced a gardener one may have been, there are so many differences that one becomes a beginner all over again. That is why I began making notes in the very first year of working in this new environment. I made notes for my future reference, but more importantly, I did it in the hope that what I was slowly learning might help others with similar problems, not only the "oldies" but to the young couples who are starting literally "from scratch."

Although this book has been written primarily to help dwellers in apartments, condominiums, townhouses and units (or whatever name yours may rejoice in), there are still many balconies in what I have called the "down-to-earth" category—that is, house and terrace-house balconies with a garden just below to replenish supplies of plants and to conveniently hide spent ones. Such areas can become places of great beauty and relaxation.

How to Define a Terrace

The word *terrace* must surely be one of the most elastic in the English language, stretching as it does from varying-sized balconies to almost any-sized level area of ground, even to the marvelously engineered Oriental rice and tea terraces; then up it comes again to describe a group of row houses, many enjoying a renaissance of popularity in recent years. But even these terraces are concerned with growing things; many small, jewel-like gardens can be seen at both front and back, and these little houses almost always have the added bonus of balconies!

I believe that most of what I have written here will also be of help to those of you gardening on down-to-earth terraces (ones less than jewel-like), but you can ignore the chapter on the problems of water-ing, you lucky ones, who can spray and splash water about with a hose, with no worry about giving offense to neighbors living beneath.

Although this book was initially tentatively titled *Balcony Gar-dening* I was reminded on a recent return visit to New York (that ancestral home of the highrise) that balconies there, when they are a little larger than usual, become "terraces" even though they may be twenty or thirty stories above the ground, just as in Hawaii the term "lanai" is applied to any balcony of any size even though the original definition of a lanai, according to my Hawaiian dictionary, is "a porch, verandah, temporary open-sided roofed structure near a house." And now here in California, it is a "patio," where at age eighty-seven I am still gardening and learning.

So let us abandon this futile effort to define a balcony and ter-race, and get down to the "nitty-gritty" of making whatever space we have at our disposal—whether it be down on good old Mother Earth or many stories up in the sky—as beautiful as we can, and if I have been able to help in any way toward this end, I will not have toiled over this book in vain.

CHAPTER ONE

Choosing Suitable Plants

We all have our favorite flowers and plants and will naturally think of them first when starting a new balcony garden, even if it is to be only a small one. Sometimes the location of the balcony happens to be suitable for the plants we want so much to grow, but when space and choice of aspect are necessarily limited, a certain flexibility could possibly avoid some disappointments (not to mention expense). Most plants are fairly expensive these days, and not all balconies have suitable places for raising seeds.

There must inevitably be a good deal of trial and error in this matter because, even when the aspect seems right, factors such as pollution from car fumes could present problems, and even when this does not arise, one sometimes encounters a baffling refusal to grow subjects that are generally regarded as extremely hardy. Geraniums are a classic example of this. For so long, they have been regarded as the perfect balcony plant, resistant to the greatest neglect and conditions that possibly no other plant would tolerate, yet I have seen ardent geranium lovers almost in tears at their inability to achieve

1

even reasonable results despite the greatest care when these plants are just not in their proper element.

Sometimes moving temperamental plants just a little distance away from one location to another will spark a response. If you do suspect pollution from car fumes is the problem, spray your plants at least every day and more, providing the sun is not shining on them at the time. This spraying (explained more fully in chapter 5) is extremely important in any case, in order to keep leaves free of the dust, which is inevitable in even moderately crowded urban or suburban areas. Plants breathe through their leaves and many also take in nourishment from such spraying, quite apart from the fact that they obviously look a lot better when they are clean.

It is a good idea to look carefully at gardens or potted plants in your area, noting which varieties seem to grow well. This could serve as a rough guide to plants likely to succeed. Every location has its own microclimate, and you must choose plants to suit it. In the world of plants, there are so many just waiting to be tried that you should not be discouraged if some favorites will not grow in your area. There are, of course, many plants that will thrive in just about any conditions: the hardy philodendrons, *Ficus* species and all the foliage plants used so often for indoor plantings. These can form a very good background in the shaded areas and will fill in very well when flowers are scarce.

Collection of primroses and assorted potted plants (Santa Barbara patio).

When choosing flowering plants, try to concentrate on those with a long flowering period, such as the bougainvilleas, in preference to those flowering only in spring. Kurume azaleas, for instance, are not of much value for balcony use because their flowering period is short, and their foliage is not sufficiently attractive to justify a year-round position when space is limited. Some of the Belgian double varieties, on the other hand, will give many months of bloom if the location is ideal. In the case of spring-flowering bulbs however, this short blooming period will not matter, because they can be dried and stored after flowering, and, of course, annuals are simply discarded after flowering. For those fortunate enough to have a near-by relative or friend with a garden, life becomes a great deal simpler because plants that are not especially attractive after flowering can be heeled into the soil until the next year, and even items in pots can benefit from an occasional change of scene and possibly additional sunshine.

Section of glasshouses at Keukenhof Gardens, Holland.

I have a friend with a large orchid collection who rents a space in a nursery into which his out-of-flower orchids are installed until the time comes for them to bloom again. The deal presumably also includes care and feeding during this time. There are, of course, nurseries that will keep up fortnightly supplies of orchids or other plants, and this arrangement may be useful for people too busy to tend the plants. But it would be far too impersonal for those who enjoy caring for their very own plants, and who become attached to them.

So if you are in this latter category (I think that you would not have bought this book if you were not) and if you have found that there is one type of flowering plant that appears to be happy in a particular part of your balcony, consider having a massed display or a small grouping of this variety, possibly in different colors, rather than the somewhat "spotty" effect of a number of different plants mingled together. If possible use the same type and color of containers. If geraniums are happy with you, then think in terms of a corner stand or a set of shelves filled with only geraniums. All red gives a wonderful impact.

Or if roses are your long suit, then have all roses, even if space may dictate only the smaller types. What could be lovelier than a collection of uniformly potted adorable little fairy roses? For the fortunate ones with the right conditions for gloxinias, the marvelous colors of these gorgeous beauties are wonderful in a mass, and the same protected hour-or-so-morning-sun position would then be ideal for the marvelous long-flowering cyclamen to carry on during the winter while the gloxinia bulbs are resting.

I know someone who found that the tricky but lovely little African violets grew beautifully in her glass-enclosed balcony. She very sensibly concentrated on these, procuring a special stand to go near the window and another trolley-type mobile stand with special lighting on which these beautiful little plants are grouped closely in an absolutely dazzling array. They flower most of the year under these ideal conditions.

This individual grouping also aplies to a collection of bonsai, which look far better kept to themselves than when interspersed with other plants. Whatever your climate, *Gloxinias.* there will be bonsai that you can grow. See chapter 17 on this.

In my case, having learned that bougainvilleas and dendrobiums were the plants to be grown here, it soon became apparent that by far the best effect to be had from the former was to keep them by themselves at the warm end of the west-aspected balcony and so I found that by putting them into small pots I could fit quite a number on a little cart. I am able to keep up a succession of color there by relegating those not flowering to another place, and replacing them from my 'reserve' corner. Fortunately, the dendrobium orchids decided that they liked the corner of the living room, where windows on either side and the door to the balcony gave them plenty of light and a good deal of both morning and afternoon sun. It soon became apparent that the corner stand looked far better filled with only these orchids than with a mixture of these and calladiums, and so the calladiums were placed all together on the floor in front to create their own massed effect.

It could take quite a few months of experimentation to ascertain just which subjects prefer just which locations, for these "microclimates" can exist even in the small space of one small balcony, but, as Don Watson puts it in his delightful book *Plants Are for People,* "It's bigger than you, this microclimate, don't fight it, use it and enjoy it!"

CHAPTER TWO

Containers

Providing the best possible containers for growing plants is every bit as important to their appearance as is the selection of a suitable vase for a flower arrangement. After all, your plants can certainly be expected to last a great deal longer than any flower arrangement!

Plants grown as bonsai provide the best possible illustration of the importance of harmony between plant and container. Take any one of those beautifully proportioned little trees growing in its shallow round or rectangular bowl and put it into a dreary black plastic, or even an ordinary red clay pot, and most of its beauty is lost. Unfortunately, most of those glazed Chinese and Japanese pots and bowls that do so much for bonsai are far from cheap, although their beauty and durability make them well worth the additional outlay. There are now many very attractive and less costly plastic and locally made pottery containers to be had. I have even seen a plastic reproduction of the traditional shallow dark brown rectangular bowl so often used for high-grade Japanese bonsai, and, until one picked it up and realized how light it was, it was impossible to detect the difference.

Planters

In addition to the pots meant for direct planting (drainage holes are provided) there are many good "planters" into which growing plants can be set in their existing pots, thereby dispensing with the need for a water-catching saucer. One very good type has a small sunken area at its base with a sort of small framework on which the pot rests, so that water draining into the base of the planter is kept below the base of the pot. Provided that the water level is monitored so that it does not come up to the level of the plant's roots, these planters can provide very valuable humidity in hot weather. The same effect can be produced, of course, by putting a layer of small pebbles or gravel in the bottom of the planter, and this too overcomes the danger of having the plants standing in water for long periods.

You will probably find that very often, especially if this desirable layer of pebbles is provided, the black plastic pots in which most plants are sold will show an ugly too-high rim above your planter. This is not an insuperable problem, especially as most nursery-grown plants are set quite low in these pots, and there is quite often a $3/4$- to $1 1/4$-inches (5- to 8-cm) space between the top of the pot and the top of the soil. It is easy to cut away most of this surplus using a sharp kitchen knife. Tie a piece of string or wire around the edge to be cut so that it will be even. If the plastic is hard, warm the knife in boiling water first. Do not cut right down to the soil level, as you will naturally need to leave a space for retention of water, but this space need not be too deep if you put a layer of sphagnum moss on the soil surface as recommended in chapter 5 on watering and drainage. About $1/8$ to $1/4$ inch (1 to 2 cm) of pot rim above the top of the sphagnum moss should prevent overflow of water and give enough grip for lifting the pot out of its planter.

Wastepaper Baskets

To hold the larger-sized pots, plastic bucket-shaped wastepaper baskets in plain colors can be quite effective. There is a type somewhat narrower than the conventional bucket, but similar in shape. These can be either used for direct planting by simply cutting a hole in the bottom with your kitchen knife, or as holders (or planters) to contain pots. As they are quite deep, it will not be necessary to cut down the sides of the pots that they are to hold; they may even be too deep, but this can be overcome by raising your pot on an inverted saucer or a shallow round margarine container, which will fill up the unnecessary depth and serve the same purpose of the layer of pebbles already mentioned.

A search of the supermarkets and department stores will reveal some quite attractive wastepaper baskets that could serve in this way. You can even use the cheap rectangular deep ones in places against the wall where space is limited and a roomy container is needed for an assortment of plants. Cut a hole in the bottom and plant directly into the wastepaper baskets. Saucers to go underneath can be a problem as round ones will not fit, but painted metal rectangular cake tins will make unobtrusive saucers that take up a minimum of space. If the wastepaper basket you choose is metal, it is not too difficult to cut the necessary drainage hole with an old-fashioned can opener. Metal and plastic can be painted to match your color scheme.

Troughs

There are many types of troughs to be found these days and, if these are weatherproof, they can be very useful for holding several pots. They are not usually very deep, so if the pot rims still rise too high, cut them down as much as you can. Instead of putting pebbles or saucers beneath them, get some pieces of absorbent plastic foam and tuck them between the pots (down and out of sight, of course). This material is very absorbent. I find it very useful, not only to blot up surplus water in my own two metal-lined wrought iron troughs, but also at the base of a large hibachus, in which is planted a large plumeria. The incurving edge of this hibachus makes it impossible to see whether there is surplus water under the pot, but with several fairly big pieces of foam around the sides and base of the pot you can determine if the surplus water will be satisfactorily absorbed. (If you are unable to get this foam, see chapter 5 on watering and drainage for alternatives.) The varying forms of this plastic foam can be used in a number of ways to help your plants. Incorporate some of the cut-up type sold to fill cushions with the soil in hanging baskets; it will provide useful moisture retention in areas that are not always easy to water. Also, the thin sheets can be cut into small circles and put in saucers under pots to serve the same purpose and to absorb surplus water. I also use these sheets, which can be bought in an attractive shade of green, to line the shelves of a small iron plant cart on which are kept small plants and bonsai. The saucers beneath these are rather shallow, and water can easily spill over the edges unnoticed. With this lining of foam, I know that if this happens I am not likely to be guilty of subjecting my neighbor downstairs to dripping water.

It is also possible to use some of the new polymer crystals either directly in the soils or around the base of the planter to absorb excess water and make it available for the roots to use later. These crystals are available at most garden supply stores. If you decide to use polymer crystals, make certain to use ones specifically designed for garden use. There are a number of types on the market. Some are more powerful than delicate root systems, stealing much needed water from the plant roots.

Cans

One of the balcony gardener's most troublesome tasks is coping with plants sold in those half-rusted cans to which nurseries still cling despite the growing popularity of plastic pots. Unfortunately, the plants that are often the most attractive are frequently grown this way, leaving one no choice but to wrestle with the problem of getting the thing open upon arriving home. Sometimes it is possible to find a helpful salesperson who will cut down the sides of the can, but if you do not have your new pot ready, or if the soil is very loose, the plant could suffer in the meantime. However, if it is not a very delicate one, and the salesperson will cut down the can, wrap the whole thing in a piece of plastic, or a plastic bag to prevent too much soil from escaping.

Repotting

Possibly the best method of removing the plant from a can is to start at the bottom edge of the can where there are usually two or three holes; insert an ordinary old-fashioned can opener into each hole and cut upward. In this way, the rim will not present so much of a problem as when trying to cut from the top. Of course, if you happen to have a stout pair of tin snips, they will cope without any trouble.

Do not try to get the plant out with only one cut down the side of the can; you will almost certainly damage its roots. For small to me-dium-sized plants, two cuts will usually suffice, but three will be bet-ter for the larger sizes, allowing you to lift the plant out with its roots un-disturbed. This is very important in the case of such tender-rooted plants as daphne, hibiscus or bougainvil-

Cyclamen.

lea. Larger trees that are bought in straight-sided round drums can often be extracted by allowing the soil to dry, then running a long knife around the edges to loosen clinging roots. Trickle water around the edges only and let the plant sit for an hour. Then give more water and leave it to soak in for a short time. Lay the plant on its side. Tap the drum all around and gently pull the plant out. You may need one person to pull while another holds the drum. As always, the plant should be well watered once it has been put into its new pot.

This procedure may also be followed when repotting a root-bound plant into a large container. But if it is small enough to invert, it is best to try the following method first. Spread your fingers across the top of the pot on either side of the main stem, then tip it upside down and tap the edge against the edge of a table or shelf. The ball should then tip out, especially if it is on the dry side or only slightly damp. With a second person to help, this can often be done with fairly large plants if they are not too tall, or alternatively, they can be laid on their sides and the tapping done lightly all around the sides. In the case of breakable containers, be sure to have some kind of padding beneath. The roots of many plants tend to cling to the sides of cement pots. To avoid this happening in the case of a quickly growing plant that you know will need repotting again, it is quite a good idea to line the sides of the container with a sheet of plastic, thus ensuring that it will slip out quite easily. Take care that the plastic does not block the drainage hole.

Do not be concerned about the roots that you may sever around the edges of root-bound plants when running the long knife around to loosen them. This is unlikely to cause much injury. It is desirable to loosen and more or less "tease out" such roots, especially those at the base of the plant, in order to prevent them going round and round into a tight ball, which will eventually become self-strangling.

Try also to shake out as much as can be safely removed of the old soil, and use only the best quality you can get for replacement. The new soil should be quite dry when you are working it down into the roots. It will then penetrate between them much better than if it is at all damp. Tap the pot up and down to make sure that there are no air spaces, and only then give the plant a good soaking. Do not just water the top, but stand the pot in a saucer of water deep enough to allow all of the soil to become moist.

The University of Hawaii College of Tropical Agriculture has discovered that poinsettia cuttings planted in white or light-colored plastic pots develop weak roots as opposed to the strong roots of those cuttings in dark green or black plastic pots. If this is true of poinsettias, it could possibly apply to other cuttings and plants. Therefore, it could be that the clear plastic pots now on the market may not provide the dark conditions that roots need to develop. This is certainly worth considering when choosing pots.

CHAPTER THREE

Wind Control

Wind is almost always the balcony gardener's greatest problem, and it is unfortunately one of the most difficult to solve, especially in the light of the many restrictions placed by councils and often by apartment and unit committees on the enclosing or even partial enclosing of overly exposed balconies. Such restrictions are understandably necessary in cases in which balconies are likely to be converted into extra bedrooms, which could overload the allowable floor space in large buildings, but it means that we, and our plants, often have to be deprived of what could be a useful and decorative protected garden area.

Plexiglas

Sometimes a partial solution can be found by backing overly open railings with sheets of heavy clear

Glass screen to protect azaleas and other small plants.

11

Plexiglas secured by a light frame, or using a lighter weight of Plexiglas woven in and out of straight upright railings. Being almost completely invisible, this will offend nobody and will certainly give wonderful protection and added warmth to lower-growing plants.

Gates, Doors and Trellises

A decorative iron gate or a not-too-high screen door or trellis secured to the balcony railing at the most windy end will break much of the force of the wind and can also provide a framework to support potted vines or espaliered plants. When wiring such screens to your railings, do not use a metal that might have a corrosive effect on the existing metal railings. For instance, if the railings are of aluminum that is not anodized, they should not be in contact with copper or galvanized wire. If they are anodized, no harm will result, but it would be wise in any case to use covered tie wire to avoid scratching. (See chapter 13 on camellias for suggestions for an espalier to train on this type of screen, or against the lower railings if they are not enclosed.)

It is possible to sometimes find decorative garden arches of either a wire or wooden trellis, which, if not too wide, can be placed at one end or in the front of a balcony. The space between the two sides of the arch can be filled with a backing of either similar trellis or a large sheet of Plexiglas so that vines can be trained over the arch with the open front providing a shelter for hanging or tall standing plants. This enables me to grow quite a number of cattleya orchids, which are thus protected from too much sun and wind, but many types of hanging plants may take the place of the orchids in cooler areas. Such a situation would be wonderful for baskets of the lovely annual *sehizanthus* (sometimes known as "poor man's orchid"), which comes in a beautiful variety of colors, but petunias, geraniums and many others would be equally attractive. The baskets can hang, not only from the center of the arch, but also from the stays at the sides. They can be secured by either wire rings that hook on or by handy metal clips made to be clamped to the rims of pots.

Chicken Wire

I once saw a balcony completely enclosed with wide-meshed chicken wire. This had originally been put there to prevent small children from falling over, but after the children outgrew this danger the wire remained as a support for two decorative but not-too-leafy vines that served to break the force of the wind and to screen out an unattractive view. This leafy screen gave a delightful effect, not only to the balcony area itself, but also when viewed from the rooms beyond. Careful trimming was done from time to time so that the vines did not shut out too much light from these rooms. The type of vine to be used in such cases depends on the climate, but there are many annuals and perennials suitable for every area. (See chapter 15 on climbing plants for suggestions.)

Plant Selection

Where it is not practical to attempt any enclosures, consider having decorative but sturdy trees and shrubs. Many of the evergreens such as the pine family and the so-called pines, including the Norfolk Island pine, will withstand quite an amount of wind. This Norfolk Island pine from the "windswept island" for which it was named can be found in a wide range of climates. It looks attractive year-round, and of course, it is very useful at Christmastime! When everyone else is scrambling to secure a good-looking cut tree, all you have to do is lift yours in from the balcony and go to work with the tinsel and baubles, which sit so well on its beautifully spaced branches.

When these trees grow tall, care must be taken that they are not blown over in very windy weather. This of course, applies to all tall trees. It is wise to pot such trees in cement or heavy pottery containers, and to crock the drainage hole with some pieces of cement to give added weight. Then put some heavy stones on the soil surface

Flowering tree from the New York penthouse of Stewart Mott.

around the trunk. This will give solidity and help to conserve moisture. Look for decorative stones in nurseries or garden suppliers. These can be either the round water-worn ones or the rough, weathered kind from mountain regions. These stones not only have the advantage of giving weight to the pots but will also prevent root damage that could result from the trunks being blown about and loosening roots not otherwise held down. Tying the trunks to balcony railings with covered wire will also help to hold them steady. In cases where there is a cement or brick wall instead of a railing the stone-weighting method is best. If trunks are tied, always be sure to put a small piece of plastic or foam rubber against the trunks to prevent damage by rubbing. (See suggestions on other wind-resistant trees in chapter 8.)

CHAPTER FOUR

Using Your Wall Space

Even the smallest balcony can usually be counted upon to have a reasonable amount of unoccupied wall area. This can be invaluable for accommodating a wide variety of plants, especially the trailing types, which can otherwise be difficult to place. Very often plants on walls will be more protected from the winds that can make life difficult for apartment dwellers *and* their gardens. Quite a number of the more delicate orchids and ferns that I could not otherwise have grown have flourished in these more sheltered conditions. Providing the means of support is the biggest problem. It will be necessary to obtain or borrow an electric drill to make holes large enough for strong plugs into which hooks can be screwed or, better still, screws long enough to attach a length of trellis to the entire wall.

Trellis

Trellis enables one to hang any number of pots, yet it requires only a couple of strong screws to support a large section. If you are not able to buy the trellis already painted, it will look best painted white.

Sometimes trellis is made of rather rough redwood slats, which looks fine on a brick wall, but for white walls it is best to search for the

painted kind. In fact, you may have to settle for dismantled garden arches. Some of these arches are in three sections, which are intended to be screwed together. Assuming the top section is straight and not curved, you can use all three sections flat on the wall. (When we ran out of wall space, I found a narrower arch with sides rather like small ladders and put that up on one of the more protected balcony corners, thus providing a little space for cattleya orchids, which needed to hang clear of the wall.)

Hanging plants allow a three-dimensional design.

A very useful type of trellis is the concertina type, which can be opened and spread to whatever width is required. These provide a wonderful amount of hanging space and are very decorative when used as support either for climbing plants or for hanging pots.

Holders and Hangers

It is usually possible to find several sizes in the ring-type wire holders for pots, and you may be able to get clip-on hangers that clamp to the rims of the pots. In order to catch water, it is best to buy the larger ring-type holders so that they can take a light plastic container for the pot. (Be sure to check on these so that water is not retained too long.) However, if you are using the clip-on type hangers, it is still possible to catch the troublesome water overflow by encasing the lower half of the pots in those circular food covers (like little shower caps) that can be bought in sets. You can make these quite easily from strong clear polythene by simply cutting circles, then hemming them on the sewing machine and running thin elastic through to gather them up to the required sizes. It is then possible to see when there is too much water in the little bags. In the meantime this surplus water, being clear of the roots, is able to provide useful humidity. It may be necessary in cold weather to watch out that too much moisture does not collect. I have recently tried out this idea for a few hot summer months, so I cannot vouch for its success in really cold climates.

Also, you can buy containers with clip-on saucers to take any overflow. Sometimes it is possible to get long, narrow rectangular trays that can be used under a narrow trellis, thus avoiding the need to catch water from every pot. These are very useful in providing humidity.

Wrought-iron Brackets

Where there is not enough space to take any form of trellis, it could be worth visiting specialists in wrought iron to look for attractive iron brackets, some of which will take several plants. These too are very decorative. I have also seen flat-backed hanging baskets designed for outside walls. These look good placed in groups. Wrought-iron brackets can also be used for hanging baskets, and there are now good-looking plastic hanging baskets in several sizes with built-in saucers both in white and various colors. (I use these quite a lot without the wires to hold standing plants, as the clip-on saucers are such a convenience.) They are certainly a vast improvement on the old wire type, which often create water-overflow problems. They also make it easier to use fiber hangers.

Plants grown in espalier fashion can look very attractive on either large or small wall areas. The range of suitable varieties is great, restricted only by your particular climate. Many plants usually grown as bushes or shrubs will take very kindly to being grown flat against any support, and many look even better this way. A classic case is fuchsias, which are thus given more of the protection they need. This applies also to camellias and quite a number of colder-climate varieties. For the hotter regions, bougainvilleas and hibiscus will catch more of the sun they love if flattened in this way, as will jasmine, gardenias and all the colorful tropical foliage plants.

Shelves

I once saw a fairly wide balcony where a beautiful massed garden effect was created by having a series of long narrow-stepped shelves built up against the wall on a framework of concrete building blocks. It was somewhat like a narrower version of the gay flower sellers' stalls that are sometimes seen in Europe or in flower markets. This may be used at one end of a balcony where there is often a blank wall. The steps can hold a wonderful array of different plants to be varied according to the seasons. If you do not wish to take the shelves down to floor level, the lowest shelf could be moved a foot or more up, with a light timber facing to hide the supporting blocks. It may even be possible to have one or two sections of this facing made to pull out like a drawer, where implements and other items could be stored. The shelves can extend almost to the ceiling, giving room for a beautiful tiered effect. On a much smaller scale, an old stepladder can be painted and used with its steps fully opened, and a series of plants placed on each step.

Fuchsias and assorted plants at one end of the author's Santa Barbara patio.

Lighting

If you can possibly manage to have a small ceiling floodlight mounted above these stepped shelves, it will prove to be the best possible investment, not only for the great added enjoyment you will have from seeing your plants at night (and of course the colors are much intensified and "glamorized" under artificial light), but this light will also help in giving extra growth and flowers if it can be left on for a few hours each evening. Daylight can be prolonged on short winter days, especially if the special Gro-lux bulbs are used.

All gardens, even the tiniest balcony ones, should be given the benefit of lighting, especially in homes where they can be viewed and enjoyed from the living rooms. Even the most common plants and flowers become beautified and transformed under a spotlight or a floodlight. This can be demonstrated by bringing plants indoors and placing them under reading lamps. There are a number of portable lights, some designed for use for barbecues and special outdoor occasions, which will adapt quite well to being hooked up on a bracket or large hook, or even to standing on the floor and tilted upward— then you will not have to install special wiring.

CHAPTER FIVE

Watering and Drainage

It is impossible to stress too strongly the importance of correct and careful watering of balcony plants, not only from your plants' point of view, but also from that of the neighbors in apartments below who can hardly be expected to react favorably to being subjected to sudden showers or even drips from above!

If your balcony is a concrete or brick parapet, there is a good chance that there will be some kind of gutter or depression at its base for drainage of storm water. Surplus water from potted plants will naturally drain into this gutter, and you will have no further problems. But for those with open-type balconies with either iron or aluminum railings, things become much more difficult, especially as the floor will surely slope slightly outward so that any spilled water will be over the edge before you have time to mop it up. Therefore you have to ensure that there are no spills.

Sources

The first and obvious answer to this is the provision of a saucer under every pot. The saucer should be deep enough to take a good deal of overflow. But it is sometimes surprising how easy it is to misjudge the amount of water that will drain away from even an apparently thirsty pot, and only experience will help you to judge this. It will help, however, if you can form the habit of going over the plants twice, giving a small amount of water the first time, then doing the rounds again with a second application if there does not appear to be any overflow in the saucer. This will take more time, of course, but not as much as it will take to have to carefully empty overflowing saucers and to mop up the water from the surrounding floor area.

It is not always easy to find suitable saucers to put under your pots. Those of cement and clay will often be porous, tending to mar the floor beneath, so generally speaking, plastic is the best. For the very large pots, one can often find small round trays. For rectangular pots, such as the ones used for bonsai, try using the oblong compressed foam trays that hold supermarket vegetables and meat. These are surprisingly durable and washable. The square ones can be useful also for either square or round pots and, by the way, these take paint beautifully. I usually paint them black, which stays clean longer than white. Painting also helps to strengthen these trays.

Other food containers can be pressed into service too. I have found that a wide, round margarine container is very good for holding medium-sized plastic orchid pots. The water drains down to the tapered base, allowing the pot to sit clear and yet to benefit from the condensation from the small amount of water beneath. The base can also be filled with pebbles to produce the same result. Sometimes plastic lids, if not too shallow can be used. Round

Two beautiful elephant stands at the Hong Kong home of Sir Kenneth and Lady Fung are a feature of their terrace. Photo by Sir Kenneth Fung.

margarine containers are useful as saucers under small pots. When inverted they also serve very well to elevate most sizes of pots that may be too shallow for their planters or troughs. There is an added advantage in perching pots in this way—it ensures that their bases will not be standing in water, yet if there is some surplus water in the planter, it can provide useful humidity without the danger of the plant suffering from "wet feet."

Azalea in the early stages of being a bonsai.

Watering Can

A can with as long a spout as possible is an essential. The sprinkler will usually have to be discarded, as these make it too difficult to direct the water into the small space of a pot. Generally, metal cans seem to be the most satisfactory. Some of the plastic ones have somewhat unsatisfactory pouring spouts.

Hoses

There are now a number of hoses available for patio plant watering. They attach to a kitchen or bathroom sink (since most balconies and patios do not have outdoor water spouts). I do not recommend these hoses. One must attach them to the sink, then run the hose through the apartment to the balcony. It seems that the pressure of the water leaving the hose is never right. Plus one has the additional problem of finding a place to store the hose.

Sphagnum Moss

I have found that my watering has been greatly helped by putting a layer of sphagnum moss (sometimes known as "florists' moss") on top of each of my plants. This keeps the plants more moist and also absorbs water better than plain soil, and transmits it gently to the plants as the soil immediately below the moss will be moist enough to absorb the water readily. I discovered this method after a heavy and prolonged rainstorm had spattered a great deal of soil out of my pots and made a horrible mess all over the balconies. Now, no matter how heavy the rain, it does not beat directly on the soil and only water, not mud, has to be mopped up when surplus water overflows. The overflow can be caught by a series of strips of old towel or some absorbent material, the end of the strip being put into the saucer. This method alleviates the heavy work entailed in lifting very large potted plants and trying to empty their saucers. Obviously such methods only have to be employed after periods of very heavy rain.

Sphagnum moss also serves a useful purpose in indicating whether or not water is needed, as it is not always possible to determine this in the case of soils that tend to cake or that are dark in color. It is not necessary to have a heavy layer of this moss; just enough to cover the soil surface will usually be sufficient. In colder climates, too much moss can result in the retention of more moisture than is needed. If the moss is at all damp, do not water. Remember too, that the rule of not watering in the late evening during cold weather applies as much to potted plants as to those in the open garden. Early in the afternoon is the best time in winter, even though the sun may still be shining on the plants. Do not, of course, water the leaves or flowers while the sun is shining on them, but watering the soil, especially if it has this layer of moss to prevent its caking, will do no harm.

In hot weather, evening watering will be quite in order, and then too, the leaves should be sprayed, especially if one lives in a dusty area. It is essential that the leaves be allowed to breathe (apart from the fact that they look very unattractive if coated with dust). The moisture absorbed through the leaves will also help the plants' growth.

Sponges

Another supermarket treasure is the assorted plastic sponges used for cleaning. These, especially the thick ones, are invaluable for absorbing surplus water, either in troughs or planters. I use smaller pieces of these in the planters containing my orchids (*Dendrobium* sp.) tucked at the sides of the pots and under pots on the high shelves of plant stands where it is difficult to look into the planters to check for surplus water.

Atomizer

Undoubtedly a most important piece of equipment for any balcony gardener is a good atomizer. This will be needed in many ways, whatever your climate. If you can get the type with a long extension, so much the better, for with this you can spray the hanging plants and those mounted high on the walls. If your garden has only a few pots, there is a very useful atomizer, made of plastic with a trigger-type handle, which gives a fine spray. I keep several of these on hand for small spraying jobs, together with another plastic type known as the "High-rise Plant Waterer and Feeder." This treasure has an 18-inch-long (45 cm) plastic tube curved at the top, with its other end in a plastic bottle, which is squeezed to eject a jet of water. It is ideal too for hanging baskets, and high-placed plants, and it is far less costly than the larger type of atomizer. Whichever type you use, however, it is very necessary for balcony gardeners to spray their plants daily, especially if you live in a dusty area. This spraying must, of course, be done while there is no sun on the plants, preferably (except in very cold weather) in the late afternoon.

CHAPTER SIX

Fertilizing

Perhaps it is in the sphere of feeding our plants that the former "dirt gardeners" have most to relearn. No longer for us the odorous, but so-effective cow and horse manures! No more of the smelly blood and bone or dried blood! Even the wonderful fish emulsion (although its devotees swear that the smell is short-lived) could perhaps be best left to the great outdoors. True, there are still some packaged forms of poultry humus that are odorless, but these are usually so pulverized that they easily blow away. They can, of course, be mixed with the top layer of soil to help somewhat, but generally speaking, these manures should be kept on the surface and not brought into contact with plant roots in the confined space of small pots.

Which Plant Food to Use

Modern science, however, has come to the rescue with a number of alternatives; perhaps best among them are the pelleted slow-release plant foods. These are not only foolproof, but they save a great deal of trouble. They give food for a period of three months. The pellets are scattered on the surface and the nutrients they contain are transported down to the roots when the plants are watered. There are now several combinations to be had in these useful pellets; 14-14-14 is the best all-round type. The numbers refer to the quantities of nitrogen, phosphorous and potash in that order. If your plants already have too much foliage for instance, you need a fertilizer with less nitrogen, so ask for one with a lower first number. These fertilizers are quite odorless and very effective. As with all food for plants in pots, do not overdo.

These slow-release plant foods are usually packaged for use with potted plants, so the directions on the containers will be safe to follow. In the case of the larger packs that are intended for use in open gardens, half the amount shoud be given for potted plants. However, it will usually be necessary to feed potted plants more often because the nutrients will tend to leach out with the more frequent watering. "Little and often" is a fairly safe rule, but not *too* often. Remember that more plants die from overwatering and overfeeding than from neglect.

When to Feed

When to feed is another often forgotten consideration. It is quite important to realize that plants, like people, need a rest period, and this is usually (unlike people) taken in winter. It is not at all good to try to force a resting plant into untimely growth at this time. Deciduous plants show quite clearly when they are resting by simply dropping their leaves, but the evergreen types do not give such clear signals. A slowing of growth at summer's end should also mean a slowing of food application. When the plants are dormant, it is best to cease feeding altogether till spring growth begins. Then you can be generous, and continue to be while growth is active because food is needed for the new growth.

While the stimulation of lush foliage growth by using spray-on foliage fertilizers can be fine for indoor plants, it must be used with discretion on those exposed to wind and sun, lest the leaves become battered and burnt. But if your position is protected, you may try using one of these. They are absorbed through the leaves and can be dramatically effective for both flower and leaf growth. Be sure to observe directions on the container, which will surely contain a warning against spraying while the plants are in the sun. Late afternoon is usually the best time. It is always desirable to spray again with clear water twenty-four hours later to remove surplus residues that could be harmful.

There are still other soluble plant foods especially made for potted plants, some to be given a few drops at a time when watering, and some to put on the soil and then watered in. All are good if used as directed. Remember that the paramount rule for feeding plants whether in the ground or in pots is that the soil should be moist before applying food in powdered, granular or pelleted form.

Citrus Trees

A special word of warning on feeding should be given to those who are growing citrus trees in pots. As I will state again in chapter 14 on citrus, it is a good idea to get special citrus food if possible, but remember that this food is usually packaged with open-ground trees in mind. In some countries instructions are given according to the age of the tree; for example, 1 $\frac{1}{4}$ pound (500 g) per year of growth. This kind of application given to a tree in a pot or tub would spell disaster! Citrus trees do appreciate small doses of poultry humus, but as mentioned earlier the light powdery material is likely to blow away.

You can overcome this by spreading it on the surface and then covering it with a layer of sphagnum moss. This will not only prevent its blowing away but gently speed its absorption into the soil. It is a good practice to have this layer on all potted plants; when there is heavy rain, the moss will also prevent the spattering of soil onto the floor of the balcony. Even though sphagnum moss is becoming rather expensive, the cost is really worth it as the moss helps retain moisture in the soil and saves you quite a deal of watering time.

Keeping Records

It is very useful to keep a small notebook in which to enter dates of fertilizer given in cases where only monthly or trimonthly applications are required, *especially* for the latter, because even a good memory can get a bit hazy after three months! In the back of the same book you can record bits of useful information, records of other people's successful results with particular plants and times of flowering of special items. Much of the material for this book came from such jottings of my own successes or failures. An index file with clippings of articles by experts on particular plants (but make sure they *are* experts), longer notes on your own experiences worth remembering for next year and nurseries and stores where various supplies were bought (how often we forget these when we want the same items later) are excellent for a larger-scale reference.

CHAPTER SEVEN

Storage of Equipment

One of the balcony gardener's biggest problems is finding a place to store items such as empty pots and saucers, bags of soil, dormant bulbs, drainage material and, worst of all, insecticides and fertilizers. Fertilizers probably create the biggest problem by reason of the unhelpful habit of many manufacturers of packaging these in nothing smaller than 5 ½-pounds (2.5-kg) bags! Often the sizes are even larger, many going up to 22 pounds (10 kg). I would very much like to appeal to these suppliers to give more thought to the ever-increasing army of balcony and other small-scale gardeners who have simply no place to store these large and often smelly packages. Occasionally a search will reveal one of the smaller garden shops where the proprietor will be helpful enough to split up the large bags of superphosphate or 10-30-10 fertilizer into manageable small plastic bags. It may even be worthwhile to propose that your local garden club suggest this course to nearby dealers. Alternatively, clubs, or possibly groups of neighbors, may get together in doing a little bulk buying and portioning out, thus saving on costs.

Even so, these items are hardly suitable for storing in kitchen or bathroom closets, and the balcony itself is the logical place. Much will depend on available space, but perhaps a small cupboard could be located at one end of the balcony. If it is low enough, plants can stand on it when it is not in use as a potting place.

Rose fertilizer.

When we bought our apartment it contained several items of furniture that we did not want to keep. One of these was a metal patio table about a yard square. Another was a mobile tray about a yard long. As this was a rather ugly brown affair, it was relegated to the balcony, under the table, which was then placed at one end against the wall. This makes an excellent place for some taller plants at the back, and the table area in front is large enough for repotting. Materials for this are kept on the tray beneath, which is then wheeled out when required and afterward goes back under the table. It has two shelves and carries pots, bags of fertilizers, charcoal, orchid mix, etc. All this is then completely hidden by a wrought-iron fire screen that fits across the front of the table and conceals a pile of larger pots and bags of soil that are too large for the tray shelves and stand at the side. I achieved an extension of the firescreen by laying another unwanted metal table on its side, with its top facing outward, and a basket containing tools and more potting material hides behind this.

CHAPTER EIGHT

Trees for Balconies and Terraces

Whatever your climate, there will be quite a range of small trees and large shrubs available for balcony conditions. Naturally the evergreen type will be more widely preferred, but even deciduous trees often have a beauty of form, in some varieties, that endures even without the added attraction of leaves. And what a joy it can be, when spring comes, to watch the rapid unfolding of leaf buds to the marvelous golden-green of newly opened leaves! It's every bit as pleasant as watching flowers open from the bud stage.

Stewart Mott with fruit tree in his New York penthouse.

Maple Trees

I am thinking, somewhat nostalgically, of the lovely delicate

31

maples, some with leaves like the finest lace. These should be treasured and given the most sheltered position you can find, for any wind will spoil them. If given shelter, or even brought into the house while the leaves are young and tender, they will make a beautiful house decoration, and will stand up to indoor conditions for months. They can then be taken outdoors in periods of calm weather. (If the tree is large, a wheeled platform is very useful.) Some of the maples are sturdier than the fine-leafed Japanese varieties: the large-leafed sugar maple *(Acer saccharum)*, the common European or English field maple *(Acer campestre)* and the box elder *(Acer negundo)* are only a few of the many varieties that grow into very large trees and will also grow for quite a few years in not-very-large pots if given good soil and plenty of moisture. The sugar maple is one of many that I grew in this way. I used to keep it in the house and on the balcony during the entire summer.

And the lovely golden-leafed *Acer japonicum aureum* with its unfolding leaves looks just like groups of half-opened fans. The leaves of this one are sturdier than most but will still tend to curl and burn if exposed to heavy wind or strong sun. Of the more than one hundred species of maple, the Japanese, smaller-leafed varieties cover a wide range of colors and forms, all of them wonderful in both spring and autumn. The best known is the common type, *Acer palmatum,* which covers the hillsides of Japan with brilliant reds and golds, drawing thousands of tourists in autumn to revel in the marvelous spectacle.

You can have a small-scale spectacle on your own balcony, and if you have shaped your small tree attractively, it will nicely blend into the background during the winter months. There are so many lovely variations of this Japanese maple that it is worth searching around the nurseries for them if you have sufficient room for several. Perhaps the most beautiful is *A. dissectum viridium* with delicately lacy serrated leaves, and this comes in a dark red form also. *A. scolopendrifolium* is almost as lovely, with longer, fine, somewhat spidery leaves. Both of these have a very graceful habit of growth. Then there are lovely foliage variations in *A. reticulatum,* with palest green leaves edged and veined in darker green, and a similar form with rosy edging. A number have dark reddish leaves, and there is a lovely medium green one with larger leaves and a more upright habit called *A. filicifolium.*

Willow Tree

Although one usually sees them in the form of very large trees, the willows can be very easily tamed into growing beautifully in either large or small pots and are easy to root from either long or short cuttings. I have had a lot of fun shaping them into bonsai and larger forms, and I greatly regret that they, like the maples, will not grow in the tropical region where I now live. In either cool or semitropical climates a cutting taken in spring, or even in summer, will root in just a few weeks if kept in a deep container of water (with a little piece of charcoal to keep the water sweet). It can then be potted into rich soil where it will continue to grow rapidly to whatever height you want. If the pot is kept in a deep saucer it will help retain the wet conditions that these trees prefer. If the climate is sutiable, the growth will be so rapid that the roots may need to be pruned twice a year. This is not difficult with such a hardy specimen as the willow. You pull the tree out of its pot (dry it off for a day or two first, as it can be a very soggy operation on a balcony otherwise) and slice off about a third of the packed roots with a sharp carving knife. I am assuming that the pot will be quite full of roots and very little soil by this time. If it isn't, it does not yet need to be pruned. Replant it in the richest soil you can get, then give plenty of water and return to the water-filled saucer. It is necessary to prune back some of the top growth at the same time to compensate for the reduced root system. Take off about a third also.

Deciduous Trees

Generally speaking, most of the other deciduous trees have a less graceful habit than the willows and maples and can therefore look less attractive when bare. This is an important point to be considered where space is limited. Where there is a big area such as in a penthouse garden, one can indulge in such deciduous shrubs as

Weigela and in fruit trees, which compensate for their bare period with lovely blossoms and fruit. For the limited areas, the best fruit trees are those of the citrus variety. So enamored am I of all the citrus that I feel I must give them a section to themselves (see chapter 14), lest this chapter become too long.

Orange trees make for wonderful balcony trees.

Taller Trees

If you are lucky enough to have a fairly large trough, it is possible to grow big trees, I was amazed when speaking some years ago with Ralph Hancock, who created the famous Derry and Tom's roof garden in London and the marvelous International Gardens on the Rockfeller Center roof, to learn that the former garden had less than 18 inches (45 cm) of soil, yet it contained a number of birches, many very large shrubs and a number of other big trees. The secret is good feeding and rich soil to begin with.

Let us turn to the taller trees and consider some that might be used to hide an ugly view or to give some summer shade. The universally popular *Ficus* genus, with large-leafed *F. elastica, F. decora, F. lyrata* and *Ficus benjamins* (weeping fig) are ideal here and can be moved indoors in freezing weather.

Ficus spp. are very amenable to shaping. In fact it is a good idea to start with a single-stemmed plant, especially in the case of *F. benjamins,* and unless you have a good deal of space, keep the side growths short because it's a weeping tree. It will look its best if grown tall, with the branches drooping downward. In the case of the choice maples, most of these are grafted onto understock of the common Japanese type, and because they are naturally soft and pendulous, they are usually already in a weeping form. The common Japanese types can be shaped in many ways (see chapter 17 on bonsai.)

Another indoor-outdoor favorite, which is also very hardy, is the Queensland umbrella tree *(Schefflera actinophylla),* which appears in a wide range of climates. This is a naturally tall grower, having strong canelike stems. It is ideal for places where you need some height.

There are many conifers, and the more compact types are very useful. I have also seen *Cedrus deodara* and several forms of spruce *(Picea)* growing well in containers. Then there is the Norfolk Island pine, so useful at Christmas! Keep Norfolk Island pines moist, but not soggy, to prevent drying out the lower branches. Spraying each evening will also help to provide the humidity they need. They are very hardy in most climates, asking only a reasonably good soil and occasional fertilizing.

Although not strictly a tree, bamboo, suitable for the warmer climates, is extremely decorative, and I have seen it used in a long trough forming a rather thick screen, blocking an unpleasant view. It will also give quite good wind protection. Also for the warmer regions, the frangipanis (*Plumeria* spp.) are ideal, especially the evergreen Singapore variety. The deciduous types are not bare for long in tropical climates. I have six different colors on my balconies. And all are a joy, giving marvelous perfumes all through the summer and standing up to wind better than most trees. Their root system is not very large, and they seem to be quite amenable to growing in small containers. Of course, the heavy top growth, with such thick branches, dictates a reasonably large pot, and there is always the problem of not overpotting newly rooted cuttings, as these will rot if given too much soil. Therefore in their early stages give them a deep—but not too wide—pot and tie the stem to the railing if possible, or to a stake.

It is possible to start big branches as cuttings, but it is important to dry these well before planting. Four weeks is not too long to let them stand in the shade outdoors before putting them into soil. If the cutting has been taken while in leaf, cut the leaves off, leaving about $^1/_2$ to 1 inch (1 to 2 cm) of stub, which will subsequently drop off. It is extraordinary how these cut branches will continue to produce leaves and flowers without any water for so long. There must be a great deal of food stored in those thick fleshy stems! They must be watered sparingly until well established. Then they can be given a general slow-release fertilizer three or four times a year.

That symbol of the tropics, the coconut palm, is wonderful on balconies for breaking the force of too much sun, or even just for decoration. They are the easiest of palms to grow, being content with ordinary beach sand, or if this is not available, any soil will do. They also can get by with a pot just large enough to take the coconut, which remains with the sprouting plant, but again there is the problem of supporting the heavy top. My two are tied to the railing, if only to hold them upright when the strong winds blow. It can be a slow business growing your tree from a coconut. It is better to buy a sprouted one from a nursery, or you may know somebody with palms in their garden, which are very likely to have sprouted nuts beneath.

A sunny patio at the home of Mrs. Janet Post in Montecito, California.

Smaller Trees

There are, of course, many smaller varieties of palm suitable for growing outdoors, but not all are sun-hardy. Again it is a matter of getting the type suited to your own climate. Some will stand reasonably cold conditions but, like *Ficus* and the camellias, would be best brought indoors when temperatures get very low. Some, like the much-used indoor palms, will not demand a well-lighted position when indoors.

For balconies in warmer or temperate areas, a coffee tree is well worth trying. It is doubtful whether you will be harvesting your own beans, but it has very pretty flowers and glossy pendulous leaves. A medium-sized tree might produce a few beans if the location is favorable, but this would have to be a very hot area. I have seen coffee trees grow well as indoor plants. They will grow quite tall if given a slightly acid soil, which holds water well, as they need to be fairly moist and must have some sun.

If possible, ascertain which of the trees you would like to grow have large root systems. Those such as the willows, as I have explained, have such fast-growing roots that frequent root pruning will be essential. The camellias, on the other hand, have a much slower and less rampant root growth and will need potting only every few years even though top growth may be quite large. Rate of growth depends on the variety. Once you decide on the variety you prefere, consult catalogs of good camellia specialists for helpful information. (See also chapter 13 on camellias.) Frangipanis too, although fast growers, do not have very big roots when grown in pots. A bay tree of any size will prove itself a great treasure. (For more information see chapter 19 on herbs.)

One of the best balcony garden trees I have ever seen was growing on the balcony of a thirtieth floor penthouse. It was an 11 $\frac{1}{2}$-foot (3.5-m) Australian weeping bottle brush.

CHAPTER NINE

Annuals for Color

Although they are inevitably transient and require a certain amount of maintenance, nothing can quite equal the gaiety of spring and summer annuals. They can be used in several ways; they can serve as fill-ins while the more permanent vines and trees are growing and can also be combined most effectively with these at any time.

The idea of combining several kinds of annuals is well worth considering. I recently saw some delightful examples of this in Europe. There were troughs with tall snapdragons at the back, then a row of medium-height marigolds, then pansies in front. In larger tubs or pots there is a lot of scope, for one can use such tall things as cosmos, lupines, delphiniums or marguerite daisies at the back, medium marigolds, snapdragons, salvia or zinnias for the next tier and in front, pansies, petunias, alyssum or lobelia. The wonderful blue of lobelia combines beautifully with many other colors, especially the bright red of geraniums, and if a border of white alyssum or candytuft is added to these two, the effect is really stunning.

Pansies

One beautiful New York balcony garden features annuals in combination with evergreen trees in tubs. Pansies are lovely used in this way; but of course pansies are lovely used in *any* way. What would spring be without these adorable masses of little faces? They are especially lovely when combined with tulips, and although this is so often done in garden beds, it can be just as effective in pots or larger tubs and troughs. The beauty of this arrangement is that the pansies hide the dying tulip foliage very effectively and then continue on their merry way right through the summer, asking only an occasional application of fertilizer and the removal of dead flowers. But if you do not live in tulip country, there are other bulbs with which this arrangement can be carried out. Pansies can combine with any number of perennial plants and flowers. There is a great variety of sizes and shapes of pansies and smaller-flowered violas, and all are lovely. They look attractive in hanging baskets too, either alone or combined with other flowers. (See chapter 16.)

Geraniums

Geraniums are almost inseparable from window boxes, obviously because they are the hardiest of flowers, standing up to a great deal of wind, sun and even neglect. The climate must be right for them, however. In areas where humidity is high and summers too hot, they can be subject to rust and will often develop a "leggy" growth, whereas in cooler areas they stay beautifully compact. Where winters are really cold, they are usually treated as annuals, and their abundance and cheapness plus the endearing ease with which they grow from cuttings make trying to keep plants in the garden all year hardly worthwhile. If you are a

Azalea and geranium.

geranium fan, it is well worth going to the shows staged by the numerous geranium societies to see the new colors and forms that appear each year. There are usually great ideas for displaying these old favorites, many of which are adaptable for balcony and terrace settings.

Petunias

Probably the closest runner-up to geraniums in popularity are the equally colorful petunias. Certainly they outdo the former in range of color and form, and they too are extremely hardy. Their perfume certainly gives them a definite edge, and even just a few in a pot can be wonderfully fragrant on warm summer evenings.

There are many new varieties and combinations of color every season. Like most of the annuals, they will continue to flower much longer if spent flowers are regularly removed. The cascade types are very good for planting around the edges of troughs or tubs to spill down, and of course, they are ideal for hanging baskets.

"Heavenly Blue" ipomoea on a Honolulu balcony.

How to Get Them

There are several ways of acquiring annuals. They can be raised from seed, either sown directly where they are to grow and thinned out later, or in shallow pots or boxes. Follow the directions on each package as requirements vary; some need no soil cover at all; others should be covered either lightly or up to about 1/4 inch (6 mm) in depth.

If you do not plan to grow enough to make seed-raising worthwhile, you can buy either small seedlings or wait for plants already in flower in small pots. This way, you are certainly able to select your colors, and for only a small number it can be worth the extra cost.

Care

Give them really rich soil when they are past the seedling stage. It is far easier to buy ready-mixed packages, as trying to make suitable mixes can be very messy on a balcony. The packaged ones are all sterilized and will contain, in most cases, enough nutrients to last until your plants are well established. The balcony gardener is usually lucky enough to avoid the slugs and snails that plague annuals in the open garden, even though there will possibly be other pests to contend with.

Use a quick-acting liquid fertilizer when flowering commences, especially after the first flush of bloom when spent flowers and stems are cut back, ready for a new crop. This cutting back can take the form of shearing in the case of small compact items such as candytuft. It will also stimulate more side growths. For this reason too, it is good to nip off the tops of the larger subjects in their early stages to encourage more compact bushy growth, even though a top bud may be closed up. Remember that, with only a few exceptions, annuals, like vegetables, need a lot of sun, but as sun will inevitably move seasonally, it may be helpful to consider using a wheeled mobile tray or stand to chase it when necessary. Where space permits, there are also troughs fitted with casters, or casters can be added to existing troughs.

Where there is only a little sun, try concentrating on such plants as cinerarias, polyanthus, primulas, balsam, impatiens and fuchsias. (Fuchsias do not grow as annuals; more details on these are given in chapter 16 on hanging baskets.) There are also a number of very colorful bromeliads, some with flower spikes and some with leaves as gay as flowers, which will grow in shaded places.

This also applies to the very attractive coleus, with its great variation of leaf shades. Some of these will require only a little sun. Experience will soon show which seem to need sun, as you will find that they acquire a drawn, leggy look if they are in too much shade.

Remember that annuals need to be kept well watered, but if you spray them from overhead, as you should do to keep dust from settling on them, be sure to avoid doing this when the sun is shining on them. Usually late evening is a good time, except at times where there is a danger of night being very cold.

Space

If you have an area with only summer sun, it could be worth investigating the idea of having a shelf attached to the railings, which will drop down when no longer needed to give more space in the sunless periods. Hinged in the manner of a drop-sided table, I have seen such shelves used for outdoor dining on narrower balconies with timber railings, but they could equally serve as seasonal plant holders. Such a shelf can also be mounted on any wall and can serve alternatively as a temporary work bench, being dropped down when more seating space is needed.

Weight

Having experienced the frustration of having a balcony end that had full sun one month and none the next, I would suggest that you consider the lightness of the containers and soil—even if wheeled carts or troughs do not fit your setting—so that lifting them from place to place will not ruin your sacroiliac. For this reason, the ready-mixed soils are much easier, as they usually contain a portion of lightweight peatmoss or other water-retaining mediums, which also help to keep the soil open.

In India, where a great many annuals are grown in the all-too-brief spring before the searing sun cuts their lives short, I have seen wonderful borders of many different plants all growing in pots, arranged with the tall ones behind and grading down through several heights to low ones in front. One ardent gardener I met had no less than two thousand such potted plants, all annuals. Realizing the transient nature of both the plants *and* the Indian spring, I asked what happened to the pots after the flowering had ceased, and it seems they are stowed away on the roof! Now while one must concede that few balconies would allow potted borders on this scale, the idea could perhaps be modified, with pots no longer occupied being stored in a garage or storage area. Plastic ones are recommended for ease of lifting and storing. (They are also vastly cheaper.)

When selecting plants to be grown, think about trying the lovely quick annual morning glories in pots with wire supports if you do not have space to let them climb. (See chapter 15 on climbing plants).

CHAPTER TEN

Roses

Miniature Roses

Undoubtedly the perfect rose for the balcony gardener is the adorable miniature or "fairy" rose, not only because of the very small amount of space it requires, but also because its blooming period is far longer than that of the larger varieties. It can be grown in any but the most extreme of climates and has actually been known to bloom quite happily under a layer of snow. It seems to have originated in Switzerland, where Dr. Roulet, for whom the smallest of the species is named, saw it growing on the windowsills of houses in the small village of Mauborget. The native people of the village assured him that it had been grown there for centuries, always in pots in the houses as it was regarded as being too small and delicate to grow outdoors. The doctor secured some cuttings that were propagated by M. Correvon of Geneva, who

named them *Rosa rouletti.* Since that time a great many other forms and colors have evolved, and it is now possible to have a beautiful collection of these enchanting little miniatures in a small area.

They show a definite preference for growing in pots: when grown in open ground they tend to lose the compact shape, which is their greatest charm. Some types grow to only 2 to 3 inches (5 to 8 cm) in height, while others will grow from 6 to 12 to 15 inches (15 to 30 to 38 cm), but all have perfectly proportioned tiny flowers and leaves.

Contrary to the belief of the Swiss villagers, these roses are extremely hardy, flower continuously from early spring until late autumn and require minimum care. In hot summers it is best to give them shade from midday sun, but generally they prefer a sunny position although they can get by with partial sun. Opinions vary as to pruning, some growers maintaining that all that is needed is the cutting off of spent flowers, taking the stems to just above the lower shoot, which keeps the plant shapely. Certainly this would probably be all that is needed for the very tiny varieties, but the taller ones could take harder cutting in early winter. Dead wood should be pruned off at all times.

Azaleas on a Sydney balcony.

Unfortunately these tiny roses are just as attractive to pests as their larger relatives, especially during hot weather, but it should not be difficult to keep an eye on them and take steps at the first signs. Easily spotted are aphids, which can be removed easily with thumb and finger from the buds and new growth where they first appear. (Do not rush for the spray gun unless really necessary.) And if, as I hope, you are spraying with water daily (after the sun has left them) a fine jetting under the leaves should keep red spider mites away. Do not spray too late in the day if weather is cold. Red spider mite is a pesky microscopic insect. It is usually green with black markings and is only red during a short period of its hibernation. It lays its eggs in a fine whitish web, and its presence is indicated by yellowish-gray blotches on the leaves. Cut off any leaves you see with these signs, and spray with soapy water (do not use detergent) and spray again with clear water within fifteen minutes. It should not be difficult to check these little plants for pests as the pots are so small and easy to lift up to check under the leaves.

They will probably be in 3- to 4-inch (75- or 100-mm) pots when you buy them, and this size should be adequate for the smaller types for a long time. The bigger-growing ones may need to go into 5-inch (127-mm) pots after a year or two, but as with most plants, it is better not to overpot. For this reason some fertilizer should be given monthly during the growing season, or failing this, give a trimonthly application of the pelleted slow-release plant food, which is scattered on the surface of the soil and gradually absorbed as plants are watered. These slow-release fertilizers are good for many plants as they have the advantage of preventing the risk of overfertilizing, especially in the case of tiny plants like these, which can be killed by overly powerful fertilizer. Whichever type of fertilizer you use, always water the soil first and water it again after applying.

Watering must also be done with care, being sure that the pot is well drained. Especially while growing, these plants should not be allowed to dry out. On the other hand they must not be watered if the soil surface is already wet. During their short resting period in winter give less water.

There have been many new introductions to the ranks of these lovely little plants since the original *rouletti* was propagated, and all are beautiful. Making a choice is hard indeed. There are pinks such as "Bo Peep," "Sweet Fairy" and "Cri Cri"; the reds include "Beauty Secret," "Zwergkonig," "Fire Princess" and "Starina." There is a lovely white 'Pixie,' with several yellows, lavender, salmon, even some with pink and white in their tiny 1/2-inch (13-mm) wide flowers. Do try to have at least one in your balcony garden, but I am sure you will want more when confronted with the task of having to choose, and certainly this is one instance when choice is not hampered by the problem of lack of space.

Full-sized Roses

If you do not suffer from lack of space, however, and still hanker after full-sized roses, there is no reason why you cannot grow these in pots. Many varieties take quite well to this. If you can use the climbing types in the background and other plants in front, the problem of their bare stems in winter will not be so great. One often sees climbing roses in pots in Italy; in one hotel in Portofino, which is famous for its flowers, large urns of roses are intermingled with ancient wisteria, all romping happily together over pergolas on a large terrace; in another hotel we saw them trained against a lattice screen. Many of the polyantha type are used on balconies all over Europe. Even quite rampant varieties can be tamed to grow as bonsai. I had good results with two old-fashioned favorites: the yellow "Banksia" (thornless, happily) and pink "Seneca Anemone."

Roots may possibly need pruning after a few years if they are planted in very small containers, but in reasonably large pots or urns they will grow for many years provided that fertilizer is given regularly. One must, however, be sure to get the right type of heavy soil for these roses, as the normal packaged all-purpose mixes are too light for the roots, which insist on firm anchorage, especially where wind is strong. Go to a rose specialist nursery for your soil if the pot in which the roses are bought is not large enough. If, after several years you feel that your roses need more space or if the roots appear too crowded and you want to plant them back in the same pots, it is no big problem to root prune them. This should be done in late winter. Turn them out of the pots, knock off old soil, and with a sharp knife or cutters, trim off 2 to 3 inches (5 to 8 cm) from the sides and bottom roots. Give new good-quality soil and water well.

Many specialists sell beautiful standard, or tree, roses in both miniature and full-sized varieties. These are grafted on tall straight stems of varying heights and look very attractive in containers.

For choice of varieties of roses to grow, it is best to go to a local nursery and be guided by their recommendations, as, like many plants, roses, while thriving in most climates, still have preferences under which they will do best.

CHAPTER ELEVEN

Bougainvilleas for Warm Climates

It is safe to say that no flowering plant can surpass the brilliant bougainvillea for use as a potted plant in areas where the climate can supply its need for hot sun. The climate does not need to be a fully tropical one; if the right varieties are chosen they can be grown in semitropical and subtropical regions (I grew a few very satisfactory bonsai specimens in cool climates), but they must be given as much sun as possible at all times.

In Hawaii bougainvilleas are in their element, especially on the Big Island of Hawaii's Kona coast, a low-rainfall area with incredibly poor-looking volcanic lava. The roots somehow thrive in this unlikely looking medium, as the bougainvilleas romp in a marvelous profusion of bloom and color. They seem able to get by without actual soil. I have bought plants from nurseries potted only in a fine gravelly mixture. Yet those I have grown in an ordinary house-plant mix also do very well, so it does seem as though the growing medium can vary widely so long as good drainage and plenty of sun are provided.

One of the best features of bougainvilleas is their marvelous adaptability to training in such a wide variety of different forms. Whether these be quite small bonsai, cascades, espaliers or standards, all can be adapted to container culture. In India, I have seen marvelous specimens trailing over balconies from large wooden boxes. A lovely garden in the Philippines features rows of uniform-sized pots along the circular drive leading to the house. And in Hawaii I know of a potted plant that has grown undisturbed for twenty-five years! This one is in a very large tub, about 16 inches (40 cm) in diameter, and it is fed regularly, which of course, is important under these conditions.

Mauve bougainvillea at this end of the balcony in the author's Honolulu home complement the colors of the orchids on the stand inside the window.

Potting

With bougainvilleas it is necessary to feed judiciously, especially in the case of smaller and younger plants. Too much food, however, can have the effect of promoting lush leaf growth at the expense of flowers. An excellent booklet on bougainvilleas distributed by the University of Hawaii advises a light application of organic fertilizer such as dried blood, bone meal and so forth, to be given to the plant when it is first planted in a container, followed by a teaspoon of 10-10-10 fertilizer per gallon container every two months after it is established. Additionally, it is advised to spray the plant once a month with a liquid fertilizer containing minor elements.

This booklet suggests as a potting medium equal parts of soil, peat and perlite, a mixture which does not compact and will ensure the essential drainage, also allowing excess fertilizer to leach out. Some experts here advise a small application of super phosphate given every two months, alternating with the feeding of 10-10-10. This is for additional leaf and stem growth. If plants are to be kept small, or in bonsai form, this does not apply. Undoubtedly plants grown in containers tend to flower better than those in the ground because the root growth is restricted.

Pruning

I have found that some varieties will flower continuously if the plants are pruned back immediately after blooming. How much pruning will depend upon whether you wish to keep the plant small, but if longer branches are required, then simply cut off the spent flower stems. Heavy pruning is unnecessary for smaller double varieties, which tend to make new buds even before the old flowers are spent, but larger singles definitely benefit from fairly heavy pruning.

Space

Where the larger single varieties are grown in prominent positions on balconies or patios, it is advisable to have them growing in light plastic pots inside the more decorative containers or troughs so that they can be lifted out and put in the background during the after-bloom period, but be sure that the background position is still one that will receive plenty of sun, for this is more important than ever at this time to ensure that the new growth will produce ample flower buds. I have found that the time taken to make this new growth will vary with different types, and for this reason, if space is limited, it is wise to be very selective in order to have the varieties that will give the longest and most continuous periods of bloom.

Cultivation

Bougainvillea cultivation will be somewhat different in the really tropical regions such as the Philippines where there is a definite "rainy season." Fertilizing, for instance, would not be a year-round affair as in Hawaii or in the warmer areas of the United States or Australia. Mrs. Luisa Perez-Rubio, who achieves magnificent results in her lovely garden in the Philippines, gave me these notes on her cultural methods:

> Fertilize with complete fertilizer as soon as the rainy season is over.... It is not necessary to mix the fertilizer into the soil. The watering will take care of transporting it down to the roots a little at a time. Repeat the process *after* the plants have bloomed, and you are ready to prune lightly, in preparation for the next blooming cycle, which should start immediately, if given the proper attention. *Do not* fertilize during the rainy season, as even if the plants want to flower, the rains will rot the buds, and this becomes an unnecessary strain for the plant.
>
> It is not necessary to water during the rainy season unless there is a long spell of two weeks during which there is absolutely no rainfall. Often times the humidity alone is sufficient to keep the plants wet. After the rains have stopped, water once a day. Do not overwater. Just allow enough to keep the plants from drying up. If little water is given, the tendency is for the leaves to fall, which then forces the plant to bring out its blooms. Once the buds show, water generously, even twice a day if weather is hot and dry as this will keep the buds from wilting, as well as prolonging the life of the flowers for a good two weeks. Heavy pruning is done during the rainy season. Prune back all branches, leaving about 12 inches (30 cm) of main branches. All small, weak secondary growth should be cut off. Repotting is done every three or four years also during the rainy season, when the plant has become too root bound and little soil remains. Then it is time to cut about 50 percent off the roots and return to the pot with new soil.

Gardeners in Bangkok confirm these cultural directions, as climatic conditions are somewhat similar. All agree that bougainvillea is the most decorative and versatile plant for a tropical or subtropical garden.

Propagation

Propagation is similar in all climates, the simplest method is by making cuttings about the thickness of a pencil and about 6 inches (15 cm) long. Remove all but the top two leaves, and plant in either vermiculite, sand, perlite or sand and peat mixed 50-1-50. Rooting will be hastened if the bases of the cuttings are first dusted with one of the rooting powders, and if the climate is dry, cover it with a plastic bag. When shoots begin to form into leaves, carefully lift the rooted cuttings into separate pots. Care must be taken not to damage the brittle young roots, which are not at all strong at the base of new plants. Keep both cuttings and newly planted pots in a shady position, bringing the rooted plants into the sun in about two weeks. When strong growth has commenced, it is advisable to keep nipping shoots back to form a sturdy, well-branched plant for the first year or so, sacrificing flowers at this stage in order to provide a better framework for later blooms.

Where climates are cooler than in the Philippines, do not follow the foregoing root-pruning advice. Where growth is less rapid remaining half the roots could be too much. I usually cut off about a third, depending on the size and strength of the plant. Certainly they make enormously long roots, but if the thought of cutting them alarms you, you can "pot on" until they are quite large, but shake out all the old soil and give a fresh lot each time.

Varieties

The question of varieties is a tricky one, sometimes varying from one country to another, but all seem to agree upon "Mary Palmer." I have seen it with this name in India, the Philippines, Hong Kong and the United States. Its popularity is not surprising, because it is the most versatile of all, adapting to many forms, but although it has a very long (almost continuous) flowering period, the flowers fall very soon. But we cannot have everything!

"Miss Manila" is a lovely salmon-shaded orange single, also long flowering, as is "Yellow Glory," a very strong grower. A marvelous red is "San Diego Red," which is also a long-flowered. I find the whites to be not as good in this respect, perhaps the best being "Jamaica White" or "Snow White." An absolutely lovely double is "Bridal Bouquet" opening with pale pink-and-white flowers, which deepen in color as it ages. I found that "Scarlet O'Hara" flowered well in my Sydney garden, and it is better suited to pot culture than most. There are several good shades in doubles, but some nurseries are very casual about names, so they have to be bought when in flower, which is a good plan anyway.

White bougainvillea.

CHAPTER TWELVE

The Adorable Azaleas

I doubt whether spring could ever be complete without the lovely azaleas. There are azaleas of almost every color and form and in such variety that choice becomes difficult indeed for the small-space gardener, but we who garden in the sky must be especially selective here,

because it is important to choose not only those with the longest flowering period, but those that will still look reasonably attractive when not in flower. Not for us therefore, the glowing orange, yellows and reds of the deciduous Mollis and Ghent varieties (lovely though their perfume can be); not for us either the evergreen Kurume varieties with their small densely packed early blooms. This

Collection of azaleas in a semienclosed balcony.

53

mass of color, as wonderful as it is, is too short-lived, and this applies to most of the larger-flowered Indicas, which make such beautiful banks of color in open gardens. However, there are varieties and hybrids that combine all the attractions of the Indicas with compactness, excellent length of flowering period and variety and size of bloom for outstripping any of their predecessors.

Hybrids and Varieties

These "new hybrids," as they are most often called, are being propagated constantly in the United States, Australia and Europe, and many are descended from the type known as the "Belgian doubles" (although many of these are actually single). This name describes those originally propagated in Belgium for the florist trade. They appear in the shops in marvelous balls of compact color in earliest spring and late winter, some even being forced, with modern methods, into flower early. They last well indoors and in protected places on balconies when weather is fairly mild.

When gardening in a temperate climate, I have been able to keep azaleas with clusters of flowers in flower from mid-winter until late summer. These were all in pots. Most of these were large flowered semi-doubles, the longest flowering being "Paul Schame," "Eri" (or "Eri Schame"), "Countess de Kerchove," "Avenir," "Pink Ruffles," "Red Ruffles" and the lovely white "Deutsche Perle." Most of these are old, well-known favorites, but there are many others and many newer descendants of all of these. There are many hybrids and crosses with these and other varieties, some with smaller, double flowers such as the lovely "Sweetheart Supreme," "Azama Kagami" and a host of others, many also long-flowering. Look around your local nursery in spring and ask which types will do best in your district, then try out a few small plants to see how they like your conditions. The 4-inch (100-mm) pot size will take up very little space and will have enough flowers to justify its being kept indoors in place of cut flowers.

Quite often, in the colder climates, they are treated like the Christmas poinsettias—that is, relegated to the trash can at the end of their flowering, primarily because subsequent care becomes a problem if insufficient space is available. But in moderate climates they should be treasured and encouraged to continue flowering by cutting off spent flowers as they fade, keeping them well watered and giving them small doses of special azalea and rhododendron food while keeping them outdoors in broken sunlight if possible. Some types will take more shade than others, but for new buds, some sun and good light are necessary. For those with clusters of flowers, it will help if not only the spent flowers are

Azama Kagami.

removed, but if a section of the stem below the clusters is removed as well. This will help keep the plant compact, and it will force new growth along the remaining part of the stem, which will, in turn, carry later buds. The flowers will last a long time if the plant is given good light, preferably near a window. If kept out on the balcony, give them a shady place while in bloom as flowers will then last longer, especially if protected from wind. When the flowers are cut back, the plants need some sun and feeding.

Containers

One of the loveliest things about azaleas is their adaptability to being changed to more decorative pots even while in full flower, and this can be an advantage if you want to have them in the living room for a time and the nursery or chain-store pot is ugly. Do not overpot them; they will remain in a small size for several years. They like fairly shallow containers as their roots are spreading.

When you do need to pot on, be sure to use an acid soil, as lime in any form is anathema to azaleas. I have often used pure peat moss if it is of good quality, but it must be thoroughly soaked first. There is usually no difficulty in getting packaged azalea-daphne mixtures. Lime-free leaf mold or mulch will help keep the soil moist. Azaleas should not be allowed to dry out, but care must also be taken that they are not left standing in water or that the soil is allowed to remain sodden. Good drainage and a layer of sphagnum moss on the surface will help if the mulch of leaf mold fails. Do not give them poultry manure. It will be too alkaline. They are not heavy feeders, and even special azalea fertilizer should be given sparingly, just after flowering.

Watch out for thrips, red spider mites or lacebugs, which will settle in under the leaves, but can be kept at bay with regular spraying under the leaves and overhead (but preferably not while in bloom). At the first sign of any of these pests, spray with soapy water, followed fifteen minutes later by clear water, but if this is not effective and you feel you must use a pesticide, let it be malathion. "House-and-garden" type sprays are suitable, but *never* use ordinary household sprays for plants.

Bonsai

Because they do well in shallow containers, azaleas lend themselves very well to being grown as bonsai or to being shaped in a number of different ways. Unless you are experienced, or somewhat of a gambler, try to do your shaping with a minimum of wiring, because the stems are extremely brittle, and you will be likely to hear a horrible "snap" on a formerly promising branch if you treat them as you would a more pliable pine. Better to rely on clipping to the desired shape, and bend branches down gen-

"Empress of India" azalea.

tly with small lead weights or tie them to a wire beneath the rim of the pot.

The type most often used for bonsai culture is the Satsuki, the native Japanese variety, also known as Macrantha type. These are winter-hardy and bloom later than most others, and here too, many late hybrids have been introduced, among them the dainty, small-growing "Gumpo," ideal for confined spaces, but with a shorter period of bloom than the Belgian types. Some of the newer ones have very large flowers, often mottled and prettily variegated, but there are lovely plain colors too.

CHAPTER THIRTEEN

The Elegant Camellias

Possibly the ideal all-round plant for temperate and cold-climate balconies is the beautiful and increasingly popular *Camellia japonica*. I specify *japonica* because the fast-growing *C. sasanqua* type, although very attractive for pot or tub culture, would eventually outgrow even quite large containers, whereas the japonicas come in many dwarf and semidwarf forms and have the added advantage of holding their blooms for longer periods than the earlier-flowering sasanquas, whose flowers tend to shatter and fall within a day or so. The fallen flowers of this prolific variety usually make a very pretty carpet beneath the plants, but while this is attractive in the open garden, it could be a distinct drawback on a balcony.

So enormous is the range of forms, colors and types of *C. japonica* that it becomes difficult to know which to recommend. They become larger and more durable each year, yet many of the old favorites are still able to hold their own, and continue to be much loved and widely grown.

Containers

A camellia could grow in a large rectangular plastic wastepaper holder, a square tub or a trough for quite a few years because they have small root systems in relation to their top growth, and as with most potted plants, it is better for the roots to be a little crowded than to have too much extra soil around them. Unoccupied soil eventually becomes stagnant, and this naturally has a bad effect on the plant. I find it better to pot them into progressively larger sizes, giving new rich soil with each potting (see chapter 2 on containers).

It is important, before making any choice, to consider carefully the place where your camellias are to be grown. If you wish to train them against a wall espalier

Gardenia-radicans in the early stages of bonsai training.

fashion, it will obviously be best to choose plants with a tall spreading habit. If they are to occupy a pot or tub near the front of your balcony, you need a more compact type that will not become too wide. Most established camellia-specialist nurseries issue a catalog that gives details of habit and speed of growth along with descriptions of color and form, so try to get all this information rather than selecting from the very tempting displays of blooms to be found at camellia shows and in plant shops.

Speed of growth is an important consideration. It is better to settle for the slower-growing varieties, assuming that you are able to start off with a specimen of reasonable size, rather than to find yourself with a beautiful, large plant that has outgrown its surroundings in a few years. Contrary to popular belief, many of the camellias, especially the newer varieties, can grow very quickly. The lovely reticulatas, for instance, have very wide-spreading branches, which make them suitable only for the open garden roomy patio locations. Many nurseries also have notes in their catalogs as to which varieties are best suited for pot or tub culture. So arm yourself with this information, and *then* sally forth to the flower shows to look at the blooms on display. If you are lucky enough to have a fairly large area of wall, nothing could be more attractive than an espaliered camellia, and the number suitable for this purpose is enormous.

The tall compact varieties are good for either free-standing positions or for growing in individual pots also against a wall if you feel that one espaliered plant occupies space that you would rather give to several other plants. For corner positions these are also good, as are the lower-growing compact types that look very attractive trimmed into either dome, ball or cone shapes, such as one sees in formal French and Italian gardens. These are decorative even when not in flower because their glossy green leaves are attractive year-round. For this reason too, these amiable plants can be put to work to provide a living screen if you need more privacy or have an unattractive area to hide, or even to help break the wind where railings are too open.

Trimming

It will not take very long to increase the density of your screen by trimming back the shoots coming out at the front of the plants, thus stimulating the needed side growths. As these plants continue to grow for much of the year, this trimming can continue until it's time for the buds to appear. Once the buds appear, do not trim the shoots again until the flowering period ends. This is the time to make any major corrections in shape or to remove larger branches if necessary. The same method should be followed in the case of the formal compact shapes, maintaining the desired shape by nipping unwanted shoots as soon as they appear rather than waiting until they grow into long stems.

Varieties

An important consideration in making the choice of varieties is also that of your aspect. Some types, for instance, will stand more sun than others. This usually applies to the reds, most of which will take more sun than pale pinks or whites, which will burn far more than, for instance, the old favorite red, "Czar." Even "Czar" will give better blooms in partial shade than in full sun, where both flowers and foliage will burn if it becomes too hot. My namesake, "Margaret Davis," a consistent prize-winner in both Australia and many areas of the United States, is remarkably sun-hardy although it is white-edged pink. Salmon pink "Hana Fuki," pale pink "Cho Cho San" and pink and white "Lady Loch" will also take quite a lot of sun. All of these are equally good in shade or semishade. Sometimes reflected heat from a white wall will have a bad effect, so keep in mind that these are shade-loving plants, preferring the type of conditions provided by protection from overhanging trees. Consider using vines suitable for providing shade. (See chapter 8 on trees for balconies for other suggestions.)

Climate

The platforms mounted on small casters can be very useful for camellias. They make it much easier to reposition the plants according to the fluctuating sunlight through the various seasons. Even with this kind of attention, unfortunately it is just not possible to grow camellias in really hot climates. Even in the relatively mild Hawaiian climate they refuse to grow except in elevated locations or the moist valleys, and even so, they only achieve moderately presentable blooms at around 3,000 feet (1,000 m) or higher on the slopes of the volcanoes on Maui and the Big Island of Hawaii. We grew some varieties quite well in our sea-level garden in Sydney, but those in our 3,000-foot-high (1,000 m) mountain garden, where winters are very cold, produced far better and bigger blooms.

Milton Brown of the American Camellia Society suggests that in areas where nighttime temperatures go below about 28°F (-2°C), keep large plants on casters or wheeled platforms so you can wheel them indoors on these very cold nights. Because the dry heat of the average apartment does not suit these plants, if you are fortunate enough to have an unheated spare room or bathroom with sufficient light or equipped with a Gro-lux lamp, you might use it for temporary shelter. Confirming the feasibility of growing camellias indoors, another member of this society, Mrs. Pat Walton, successfully grew and flowered camellias in a basement equipped with fluorescent lighting in Augusta, Georgia, and later in New Jersey in a basement with a thermopane door on the south side, which enabled the plants to receive sun all morning. The basement has a hot-water heating system, which maintains the temperature at 50 to 55°F (10 to 13°C) throughout the winter and the humidity remains high at all times. This indoor situation has enabled Mrs. Walton to avoid all insect and disease problems, and so successful has it been that she plans to leave the plants in the basement all summer.

As Mrs. Walton's plants are not large, she is able to bring them into the house when they are in bloom, and all of them bloomed in the past season. It could certainly be worth the cold-climate apartment dweller's while to take a look in the basement for unused, or unfrequented space that may lend itself to housing these very beautiful flowers. Some apartments even have reasonably large storerooms, which could be possibly pressed into service, especially those with only wide-meshed wire divisions, that can be locked. A house, of course, has many more possibilities.

It would be worthwhile to check which types seem to thrive best in your own neighborhood before making the final choice. When only a few plants can be accommodated, this careful selection will pay off in the long run because these are very long-lived plants, and it would be a pity to spend several years training your plants to good shapes only to find that they do not give good flowers.

Soil and Fertilizing

Camellias need a slightly acidic soil with a good deal of leaf mold or peat moss. It may be possible to buy special camellia soil from local nurseries or garden shops, and many firms package special fertilizers. These should be used sparingly as soon as there is any sign of growth, particularly just after flowering, but remember that amounts shown on the packages should be halved for container-grown plants. This applies to most plants. (A good fertilizer is the slow-release Osmacote.)

Watering

Keep the plants fairly moist at all times, especially when flowers and buds are forming, but do not leave them with "wet feet"—don't let water accumulate in the saucers beneath the pot. Do not water until the soil surface is dry. In very hot weather it is wise to spray the leaves in the late afternoon when there is no danger of sun reaching them. In cold climates, spray the foliage earlier in the day. Most japonicas will tolerate temperatures down to 37°F (3°C), but this is too cold for the completely double flowers, which will need to be moved to a protected place in very cold winters.

Repotting

When transferring a newly bought plant to an ornamental container, take care not to cover the roots too deeply. They should be no more than $3/4$ to 1 inch (2 to 3 cm) below the soil level, allowing them sufficient air. A light mulch of sphagnum moss, manure or leaf mold will help conserve moisture, provided it is not too deep.

Pests and Diseases

One of the greatest advantages of camellias is their freedom from the many pests and diseases that plague most other plants. Occasionally they may be attacked by scale or mites. Use an oil spray for the scale and specific oils or insecticidal soaps for mites but *use these only when it is really necessary*. Indiscriminate spraying can destroy valuable predators such as ladybugs or any birds you may be lucky enough to have. These sprays are also unpleasant and (if not handled carefully) dangerous to the sprayer.

Die-back is a disease that can attack camellias in certain areas. This is very hard to control, although I know some growers who say they find Benlate helpful. Because this is a disease that will travel quickly throughout the plant, it is advisable to cut off the affected part immediately, and to cut the stem back to where there is no more sign of the tell-tale brown in the center of the stem. It is recognized by a sudden collapse and drooping usually of new growths.

Disbudding

Many varieites need disbudding, even the small plants. The usual tendency is to remove all the smallest buds, keeping just one or two of the biggest. Instead, if you also keep one of the smaller ones, it will give you a flower after the others have finished, and if this is done with all plants, a longer flowering period will result.

Did you know that fallen blooms that are in good condition can be kept for several days in the crisper of your refrigerator? In this way they can be saved for table decoration, as one is naturally very reluctant to cut flowers from precious decorative plants.

CHAPTER FOURTEEN

The Wonderful Citrus Family

No matter how small your balcony, you can grow at least one citrus tree, for this very large family includes specimens from just a few inches high to 3 to 5 yards. Even the larger members often can be found in dwarf forms. I doubt whether any tree is more decorative or rewarding to grow. Even if the fruit is not edible, the tree is worth growing for its beauty. A well-grown, well-shaped citrus tree can outshine even the most glamorous of flowering plants. On the days I opened the garden to charity functions, admiring crowds stood around the collection of citrus trees in the terrace garden we had in Sydney. Although there were many lovely azaleas, rhododendrons,

A tangelo tree.

camellias and magnolias, it was the potted citrus trees that constantly stole the show. Many people asked, "How can we grow oranges, lemons and mandarins in tubs like yours?"

So now I am going to tell you. No matter which type of citrus you may decide to try, it will bring you an enormous amount of pleasure for many years—yes, *many* years. Even on a balcony, these trees can be kept in small pots for very long periods. Bonsai growers will confirm this, but if you prefer something not quite so small and have room for a tub, you can plan on a lifetime tree. I was once fortunate enough to spend some time in Paris with the director of the parks and gardens of that lovely city, and as his territory included the gardens of Versailles I asked about the age of the orange trees in those big square tubs that some of you may have seen. It seems that some of these are still the original trees planted at the order of Louis XIV, the "Sun King." They would, I imagine, have often been root pruned and given fresh soil in all the years between, and also would have been moved into a conservatory or "orangery" for the winter months, as is done with the citrus trees so much used in the lovely formal gardens in Italy. An Italian gardener once told me that this is why the decorative Italian tubs are so often equipped with handles—to make it easier to lift them indoors. In some of the lovely old gardens in England, we still see "orangeries," even though they will probably be occupied by plants other than orange trees.

Do not despair if yours is a cold climate and you do not have an orangery, as your plants can spend winters right in the house serving as decorative house plants. You must give them a good light, as close as possible to a window, and keep them well watered to offset the drying effects of heating. A bowl of water close by will also help provide the needed humidity. I know someone who keeps a lovely kumquat in a tub in her living room; it is right inside wide doors leading to a terrace, and these doors are open much of the day.

Calamondin and Chimoti Trees

It will be much simpler to have fairly small plants in cases where they must be moved indoors in winter, and even if your local nursery does not stock the grafted dwarf types, it is still possible to grow the very attractive little calamondin, which has different names in different countries. In the Philippines it is "calamanci," in England its name is *Citrus mitis,* but its botanical name is *x Citrofortunella mitis.* By any name, it is a beautiful little tree with small orangelike fruit and fragrant waxy flowers. Then in the slightly larger category comes the myrtle-leafed mandarin (chinoti) with smaller flowers growing in clusters all the way along the stems, and fruit, also in clusters, that stays on the tree for months. This fruit is not so good for eating, but it is so decorative that I could not imagine anyone wanting to pick it anyway. This tree is lovely in flower, it would be worth growing just for its flowers. One must search for short plants of this one, as it tends to get a stiffly erect habit if not pruned and shaped early on.

Kumquat Trees

There are several varieties of kumquat (or cumquat) and these too can be kept quite small. The one that has oval fruit, nagami, makes delicious eating picked right from the tree, but the round-fruited one, marumi, is quite bitter, although it makes very good preserves and marmalade. The beauty of kumquat fruit is that it can be left on the tree for many weeks and cut and used only when it becomes obvious that it is too ripe to remain any longer. There are also variegated-leafed forms of both of these kumquats, but with

A kumquat tree.

these, much of the attraction of the contrast between the bright fruit and the glossy dark green leaves is lost.

If you prefer the idea of growing oranges, lemons, tangelos, tangerines or mandarins and cannot accommodate large trees, go to a specialist nursery and walk along the rows of trees in search of one that has been grafted low down, or even a short tree on a normal graft. Make sure that the stem is straight however, because that is necessary if you are going to grow it with a bushy top. Although grapefruit grow beautifully in tubs, unless you have a good-sized terrace, it may be best to forego these.

Even if you plan to grow your citrus tree against a wall, espalier fashion, you should start off with a good straight stem. Citrus of all kinds lend themselves beautifully to this form of growth. If you have a sunny wall, plant your tree in a square tub or a deep trough. In either case it will be possible to attach a small trellis or some crossed stakes to give support if it is difficult to plug the wall. The purpose here is not so much to give support, because the branches are quite strong, but to train the tree into an attractive shape. Also, one of the reasons for growing trees against sunny walls is to give them the maximum of precious sun and warmth, just as it is where they are grown in gardens in many countries where winters are cold and summers short.

Orange Trees

Oranges are somewhat sensitive to climate depending on the variety; it is best to consult your local nursery before selection of a specific tree. Choose nursery trees carefully. Look for certified trees with a large root system of many lateral and feeder roots, straight trunks and leaves of a deep green color. The graft union should be 4 to 12 inches above the soil level, and the trunk an inch above the graft union should be $3/4$ to $1\,1/4$ inches in diameter. Newly planted trees need lots of water until they become established. In hot, dry areas, water young trees every two to four days. In wetter climates they will need to be watered once a week.

Citrus trees can bear fruit without pollination of the flowers, so you need plant only one tree. The fruit that develops from unpollinated flowers will be seedless.

Lemon Trees

Lemons, although not always easy to train into formal shapes, make excellent espaliers, and they thrive in a wide range of climates. The

"Meyer" lemon, that not-too-sour lemon with the orange in its parentage, is an excellent variety to grow in either temperate or cold climates. Some that we grew in our cold mountain garden at 3,000 feet (1,000 m) sailed right through frosts and snow out in the open ground, so I feel sure they would do so on a sheltered balcony.

Tangelo Trees

And do try to get, if you can, that most beautifully colored of all the citrus, the tangelo, a marvelous orange-red, and a cross between a mandarin and a grapefruit. About the size of an average orange, these highly decorative fruit remain on the tree for long periods. Taste varies somewhat according to the district and soil in which they are grown. They are less sweet than their mandarin parent and are very good for refreshing drinks. There are several

Citrus tangelo gives wonderful color to a sunny terrace. The fruit can be somewhat bitter if not allowed to fully ripen on the tree, which means that the tree remains decorative for quite a long time.

types of tangelo, one round like an orange, another more pear-shaped. All are good.

Mandarin and Tangerine Trees

Mandarins and tangerines are worth investigating. Choose the variety best suited to your climate and district. Again, look for good color. The specifics for planting all citrus tend to be the same—with the best planting time occuring in late winter and very early summer, when the trees are growing slowly. There are many varieties, and it is important to try for those with the best fruiting record. This can vary quite a lot too.

Care

If possible try to buy your tree in a plastic pot. These are so much easier to deal with than the metal cans often used by nurseries. As citrus trees do not have very large root systems, the soil in which the tree is bought should be adequate for at least three years, provided that you give regular applications of fertilizer. Most stores carry special citrus food, and this should be sufficient if you carefully follow the directions on the box. Do remember that these will be for trees in open ground unless specified otherwise, and amounts should be halved. You can also give applications more often in this case, however, as nutrients do leach out with the more frequent watering needed for pots. Poultry manure given in late winter and autumn is very good also.

Potting

If your tree is bought from open ground, that is, bare-rooted, take great care that the roots are not allowed to dry out while preparing the container. Keep them soaking in water at this time. Be sure to provide good drainage in the container by putting a curved crock or piece of broken crockery (convex side up) over the hole. You should always keep any broken cups or saucers for this purpose. Put several more pieces around the first one, and then cover these with some coarse material such as pieces of sacking, net, open bark, anything porous enough to let the water through but that prevents soil from running out. Hair trimmings are fine, and most beneficial to plants. Now fill in some soil (the richest you can get but alkaline). I always prefer to spend the extra amount for good-quality, sterilized potting soil rather than to attempt the very messy business of trying to mix and sterilize soils in confined balcony space.

It must be emphasized here that the pots for these bare-root trees should be just large enough to accommodate the roots, and they should be planted at the same depth as they were in the soil of the nursery. Over-potting of any plant is very bad. The unused soil rapidly becomes stagnant, holding too much water, and roots can rot rapidly under these conditions. It is better to repot more often than to pot plants in oversized containers in the belief that they will "grow into" them. This is one of the most common mistakes of inexperienced gardeners, who believe that they are being kind to their plants in giving them plenty of room! Make sure that the newly planted tree has plenty of water. When using new soil I always let the plant stand in a saucer of water for half a day to be sure the soil becomes properly moistened.

Watering

It is difficult to lay down rules for watering citrus. As with any plant, this will depend entirely upon the location, rainfall and time of year, but it would be safe to say that in their growing period, these trees need to be kept reasonably well watered; that is, watered when the soil on the surface seems dry, but not if it is already moist, or if there is any water in the saucer beneath the pot. Like most balcony plants, they appreciate a nightly spraying, or, if weather is cool, spray in the afternoon after the sun has left them. This will help greatly for general health, and keep the leaves glossy and free from dust.

Training

Citrus trees from open ground usually have three main branches. Treatment of these will depend, at this stage, on the shape you wish the tree to ultimately take. If it is to be spread against the wall, in either a formal or informal espalier, tie them to their supports, nip out the top of the central, upright branch to induce side shoots and tie the others almost horizontally. Do not tie these too tightly; remember to leave room for growth. As your space will probably not permit the height or length of the perfect "ladder" types seen in open gardens, it may be best to try not to be too rigid about this. Think in terms of either a fan shape or an informal spreading form. When side branches appear they should also be loosely tied to the supports when long enough. Nip out those not needed to maintain the shape you are aiming for. This should be done before they become long, of course.

When the desired main framework has been achieved, it simply becomes a matter of nipping back shoots that tend to grow outward. If space on your balcony is limited, you may have to be somewhat ruthless about this in order to keep a very "flattened" tree, but it will keep it neat and you can still leave enough length to carry some leaves and hopefully some buds.

I know some gardeners who are very strict in their training of the original espalier shapes, even to the extent of starting with just one stem, which is cut back from the usual height of around 29 $1/4$ to 12 inches (75 to 30 cm). Although this ultimately gives a better formal shape, it sets the tree back at least a year. While this doesn't matter so much when it is occupying a background place in the open garden, it does not look at all attractive in the close confines of a balcony.

It is possible to achieve a good compromise between a conventional espalier and the European round-top ideal by aiming at a flattened type of the latter—that is, keep the tree to a single stem, but instead of having a fully round top, one side stays flat against the wall and the rest is kept rounded in the usual way. This can be very effective against a white wall, and results are quicker, not only as a result of the warmth of the wall, but because all growth is concentrated toward the front, giving a more bushy effect. This form also saves space. For this, or the normally all-round shape, it is simply a matter of keeping the stem as straight as possible, using a stake if necessary in the early stages, then nipping out the shoots when the desired height is reached and keeping the subsequent side shoots nipped when they reach the shape you are aiming for. Do not be too severe about this when it is time for buds to appear, for after all, who wants to spoil the joy of those lovely fragrant blossoms, even if they are not followed by beautiful fruit.

Unfortunately, gardening in the sky does not confer immunity from pests, and it is possible that scale and aphids, which plague trees on the ground could follow them aloft. How this happens, I have never been able to discover; perhaps the eggs are already there or are carried in with other plants, but come they do. However, we do have a great advantage in being able to check our plants at close quarters, and both these pests are easy to beat if dealt with early. In the case of scale, whether it be white or brown, as soon as you see the first sign rub it off with any fairly firm brush. An old toothbrush kept on hand for this purpose should take care of it. The brown type, not so easy to spot as the white, usually clusters on the main stem. The white, which is softer and has a waxy look, will be found on the smaller branches or at the base of leaves.

Aphids' favorite spots are the tips of new shoots. For these, spray with soapy water, or dip the branch into a bowl of soapy water to wash them off. If you cannot dip them (the branch may not be flexible enough) then spray them, leaving the soapy water on for no more than 15 minutes. Then spray again with clean water; soapy water is not good for young growth if left on for too long. Above all, do not dash for the can of pesticide at the first sign of an insect. Remember that even the most allegedly harmless of these products can often have cumulative adverse effects when used in confined spaces. (See chapter 20 for more on this.)

Remember, too, that many of these pests, especially the beastly mealy bug, are conveyed to your plants by ants, those most pesky of insects, to plague balcony and indoor gardeners. If you can banish these, you can avoid much trouble. Again, try the old-fashioned methods first. Slower but safer! If you happen to see a black sooty mold, this is a forerunner to scale. Use the soapy water treatment, or scrub it off at the first sign.

Orchids and bougainvilleas.

Poinsettias and bougainvilleas.

Slipper orchid.

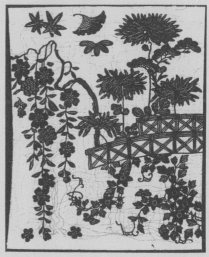

Cyclamens.

*Amazing contortions of bamboo trunk
from the balcony of Chinn Ho.*

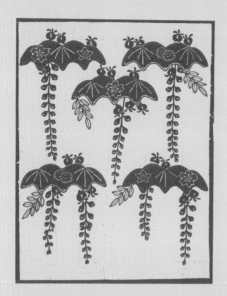

Catlleya Orchids.

"Margaret Davis" azalea appreciates a sheltered area.

Hibiscus grow well in pots only for a few years.

Kurume azaleas in abundance.

Chrysanthemum at a bonsai display in Tokyo.

Lillium rubrum.

"Countess de Kerchove" azalea.

Fuschias adapt well to pot culture.

Hibiscus and bougainvilleas enjoy Honolulu's warm climate.

Hibiscus

Gloxinia surrounded by African violet.

CHAPTER FIFTEEN

Climbing Plants

Climbing or trailing plants create a good effect even on very small balconies. Any wall is far more attractive when used as a background for leaves and flowers, and a surprising number of vines adapt very well to growing in containers, provided that sufficient support is given.

The question of plugging walls to provide this necessary support can be a tricky one if you don't own your apartment or house. If the owner is unwilling to give permission for this, you can use those small adhesive hooks often used to hold small pictures on indoor walls. These can support wires, string or even a small lightweight trellis of wire or plastic. A series of fine nylon

Philodendron scandens on the interior walls of Stewart Mott's penthouse.

cord or string can be tied around the pot in which the plant is grow-ing and linked to some small hooks where the walls join the ceiling to provide support for a vine. With luck, there might even be a wood beading there.

If you have an ugly view to shut out, or need more privacy, then a length of wire netting with as open a mesh as possible would perhaps be the best. There is no limit to the variety of vines that can then be grown. Do not choose those with a very thick growth habit which could exclude the light from the rooms beyond or from the rest of your balcony. There are many suitable vines that can be easily kept under control; the choice depends, of course, on your climate.

Ivy

Possibly the best all-around vine for this type of wire-mesh screen is ivy. It can now be found in many forms, from the well-known old English type to some with quite tiny leaves. A very quick-growing one is *Hedera* "holly," with attractively waved somewhat hollylike leaves. Ivies are best grown on wire rather than against a balcony wall because their tightly clinging roots will leave un-sightly marks if they are later removed. Also their tenacious habit of delving into any gaps in plaster or brickwork can become quite troublesome.

Fatshedera

There is a very attractive semiclimbing cross between ivy and *Fatsia* known as *Fatshedera*. It has the strong stems of its *Fatsia* parent and requires little support. From the *Fatsia* parent also come the large glossy leaves for which this plant is so greatly prized. In Japan *Fatsia japonica* appears in almost every garden. From both parents *Fatshedera* inherits great hardiness. It can be used outdoors or as a decorative indoor plant. While it is adaptable to either sunny or shaded loca-tions, its handsome leaves show better in shade. Regarding soil, *Fatshedera* is not difficult to please, but prefers soil that is a fairly rich loamy compost.

Monstera Deliciosa

Another well-known plant is the handsome *Monstera deliciosa*. Often grown as a nonclimbing plant, it will nevertheless reach any height required if given a wall or any strong support to which its thick aerial roots can cling. These aerial roots cause some concern to gardeners, especially as this plant does seem to produce many more than are needed to help it climb. And because they tend to push out rather untidily, the question is often asked whether they can be cut off without damage to the plant. Shortening a few does no harm, but wherever possible, guide them down into the soil of the pot. Even when they are quite tall, this can still be done, because these roots reach a great length. They actually take nourishment from the air, but for pot-grown plants where they are receiving periodical fertilizer, this is not as essential to their well-being as when they are clinging to the trees in their native habitat.

Philodendron

The range of philodendrons is enormous, encompassing many larger types down through intermediate sizes to the ever-popular little *P. scandens,* with its appealing heart-shaped leaves and its great adaptability to either climbing upward or drooping gracefully down from hanging baskets or from pots on high shelves. One of the most attractive uses to which I have seen this plant put was in the penthouse living room of Mr. Stewart Mott, where it grew from the walls right across the ceiling, making a beautiful pattern. The branches, which will not cling unaided to smooth surfaces, were held to the walls and ceiling in this case by small strips of white adhesive tape such as are used to hold small pictures. This little plant also blends very well with driftwood, as its leaves are small enough not to obscure the attractive wood. It must be remembered that this variety will not tolerate a great deal of sun, but on a shaded or semi-shaded balcony it can look beautiful, adorning walls or even reaching across the ceiling.

Grapevine

For sunnier balconies there are many lovely vines, both flowering and foliage types, and one can even hope to pick fruit if space

permits a grapevine. Even
without their delicious
fruit, grapevines are very
attractive, and if your balcony is too hot in summer,
the leaves will provide wel-
come shade, as they do in
the little outdoor cafes of
Italy. Italian balconies too,
make a lot of use of grapevines, often twining around
ancient fluted columns and
over lattice shelters. There
are other equally attractive
forms of grapevine grown

This assortment of vegetables on one side of a penthouse garden provides excellent proof that one can have a kitchen garden on the 16th floor.

just for their foliage, which colors marvelously in autumn. There is also
the similar and very decorative Virginia creeper, ideal for clinging to
walls and supports. Another New York penthouse uses this vine to completely clothe the walls of the apartment, creating a lovely cool
green background for the hot summers. Ivy geraniums planted
in a trough against the railing will clamber up and along the railings for a long distance, providing attractive cover.

Clematis

Possibly the loveliest of all the flowering vines suitable for growing in pots is *Clematis spp.*, with its large elegant flowers in many
colors. Anyone lucky enough to visit the English Chelsea Flower
Show remembers the displays of these lovely flowers in a wonderful range of shades and growing in not-very-large pots. As
most varieties are best cut back in winter, there is no problem
with the somewhat straggly branches when bare. Clematis prefers an alkaline soil and likes to have its roots in shade and its
branches in sun. It is only suitable for the cooler areas. Sometimes the smaller-flowered types will grow in temperate regions,
but it is happiest where winters are cold.

Wisteria

Wisteria, that beautiful giant among climbers can certainly be grown on a balcony. I have seen beautiful specimens flowering in high apartments in southern France and in Italy, usually planted in antique-looking tall "Aladdin-type" jars. Possibly these containers give the roots a good depth of soil, but repotting these plants is very tricky, as anyone who has tried to extract a plant from a container with an incurving top will know. Wisteria does need frequent repotting or root pruning, because it is an extremely robust subject. It would be possible, as the roots will themselves to be cut anyway at this time, to run a very long sharp knife around the top edge of the jar and then drag the plant out and prune away more roots from the base.

When root pruning wisteria, about a third should be cut away altogether. Cut an equal amount from the branches to compensate for the reduced root system. Shake off as much of the old soil as possible and replant in fresh rich soil. Deep, straight-sided containers or urns are very suitable for wisteria; or you can use a bar-

Pale pink and mauve wisteria on Mrs. John Bacon's Montecito balcony, growing up from the garden below.

rel cut about two-thirds or three-quarters up, and the space around the vine can be filled with flowering annuals or bulbs. Wisteria will flower well even in a small container, but it can sometimes be unpredictable under these conditions: I had to wait six or seven years for one of mine to start flowering, and the Japanese types can sometimes take longer than the more common Chinese variety. It is best to go to a nursery and buy plants already in bud to avoid this long wait. These will most likely be grafted plants; those grown from suckers, cuttings and seedlings can be very slow in flowering. Full sun is essential for this vine, and it needs a cold or temperate climate.

Stephanotis and Hoyas

Those who live in the tropics have the good fortune of being able to grow the lovely fragrant stephanotis and hoyas. All are fast-growing, fragrant and grow well in pots.

Stephanotis likes a sunny location, but can grow quite well with only partial sun. Unfortunately it is subject to attacks by mealybugs. Spray periodically with soapy water, being sure to follow this with a spray with clear water no more than fifteen minutes later. Do not leave soap on plants very long. If the mealybug is only fairly sparse, you may only have to use plain water, but once ensconced, stronger measures are needed. Stephanotis performs best if cut back quite hard after flowering is finished.

Hoya obtusifolia has a flower quite similar to that of stephanotis, but its leaves are larger, glossier, round and very decorative. This vine appears to grow as well in water as in soil, which allows for a wide choice of containers. A piece of charcoal must be kept in the water at all times. Although it will flower reasonably well under these conditions, over a long period, soil probably would promote better growth. This vine will grow quite well in shade or sun. It appears to be impartial in this respect, which certainly makes it a treasure. Another great plus is that it seems to be resistant to attacks by pests.

There are many other varieties of Hoya, perhaps the best known being the medium-flowered *Hoya carnosa,* with pinkish-beige flowers and either plain green or variegated leaves. This one grows in a wide range of climates. This does not grow as rapidly as *H. obtusifolia,* but is very hardy and useful (though it will not stand frost). When the pretty porcelainlike flowers appear you must not yield to the temptation to pick them if you hope for more flowers next year, because this plant has the strange habit of bearing its subsequent flowers in exactly the same places. So do not remove spent flower stems, as you would with so many other plants. Likewise, pruning is not advised.

Stephanotis.

Cereus

The matter of thorns must be noted if you think about planting the lovely night-flowering cereus. There are a number of varieties, some quite thornless. The one I have, which grows equally well in the temperate climates of Sydney or southern California as it does in Hawaii, is quite thornless, yet many of those rambling over walls and hillsides around Honolulu are very prickly indeed. Actually, although its flowers are very beautiful and much lauded, those of the thornless variety, known variously as "Belle de Nuit" or "Princess of the Night," *Selenicereus nocturnus* seems to be better and has the same beautiful but very strong fragrance. *S. nocturnus is* sometimes mistaken for *Epiphyllum oxypetalum.*

Cereus will grow from just a short section of stem, prefers rich soil and will thrive in either full sun or semishade. It can stand fairly low night temperatures, down to about 39 to 41°F (4 to 5°C). As the leaves and stems are heavy and fleshy, a fairly heavy pot is needed. The stems will not need much support if grown against a wall or screen as they are very strong. I have a self-support one that is about a yard tall. They will, of course, grow much taller if allowed enough space, but a larger pot will be needed.

There are other cereus that flower in the daytime, all with very beautiful flowers. Do not overlook the annual climbers, even though their life span is shorter than those already listed. They can give very decorative results. Most beloved of these are the sweet peas, and though one can hardly hope for the very tall growth of plants in the ground, a reasonably deep trough and the best of soil will produce acceptable results. Some kind of wire or string frame is needed for tendrils to cling to. Try to find the perennial variety for the best results. The great plus with annual sweet peas, however, is that winter-flowering as well as spring- and summer-flowering varieties can be had. Seed should be soaked in warm water for a day or two before sowing about $^1/_2$- to $^3/_4$-inch (1- to 2-cm) deep. Give fertilizer every month.

Clerodendron Thomsonae

Clerodendron thomsonae, often called the "bleeding heart vine," is another very decorative climbing plant suitable for balcony culture in warm, frost-free areas. It has clusters of white calyces; small blood-red flowers hang from the centers of these. Unlike the twining plants just described, *C. thomsonae* has strong stems, which can be kept short enough to grow it as a compact shrubby plant, but it will obligingly grow taller if given some support. There are other clerodendrons, but this one is perhaps most suited to pot culture. The others are robust subjects and require quite hot conditions.

Ficus Pumila

If you have a brick wall that you would like to cover with green, it would be hard to surpass the climbing member of the tough *Ficus* genus, *F. pumila*. This small-leafed and very attractive little fig will do the job very quickly. No wires, strings or sticky-tape is needed to hold this little plant in place. It has extremely tenacious sucker-equipped stems that will cling unaided—no matter how high the wall. And if your walls are not very high, the branches will proceed to meander across the ceiling. With increasing age the leaves grow larger on plants in the ground, but I doubt whether this would happen when planted in a pot. *F. pumila* has an even smaller form that is more suited for growing in very small hanging baskets, but this one is not so easy to find.

Cotoneasters and Pyracanthas

Also evergreen and sturdy, although not clingers, are the cotoneasters and pyracanthas. There are several varieties of *Cotoneaster horizontalis* (which can also be deciduous and semideciduous in cooler climates), and all are good. The rigid branches will need some support, but not a great deal, and they will create lovely patterns against a light wall. Its clusters of small white flowers and bright red berries make it very valuable for cold or temperate climates, especially in winter. Pyracanthas produce even bigger and better clusters of berries, but those I have seen have all been very thorny, which is not a good attribute for balcony culture. As there are many forms, it could be worth looking around for a thornless or not-too-thorny one, if you have a corner where it could stay in the background.

Climbing Plants for Quick Results

The nasturtiums can be used for quick results; not much coddling is needed for these. Also, if you like orange shades, the bright little *Thunbergia alata* (black-eyed Susan) grows well in containers. It can often be found in nursery pots already in bloom. It will quickly climb on a trellis or frame to give a long-flowering bright background. Another "quickie" is *Cobea scandens* (cup-and-saucer vine) with its fascinating flowers, which change from green to purple with many shades in between. Stems are quite long too, making them excellent for cutting (if you can bear to cut your balcony flowers). *Cobea* likes a sunny position. Unfortunately, it is not possible to move climbing plants about to keep up with the sun's movements as you can with compact plants. Perhaps if you know which way those precious rays are heading you could train the long growth in that direction. Often, the plants will do this for themselves.

Morning Glory and Moonflowers

Two annual climbers that I have grown in several different climates with equal success are morning glory, (*Ipomoea* "Heavenly Blue") and its night-blooming cousin, the moonflower, which is white. Both grow incredibly fast. I once measured the morning glory's rate of growth and found it to be about 8 inches (20 cm) a day! Of course, this was in Hawaii's tropical climate where this rapid growth rate unfortunately also means a far shorter life-span than in cooler climates. Even its brief glory is something to cherish, if only for being able to get close (as one *can* on a balcony) to that miraculous color so aptly named "heavenly blue." In temperate and cool climates, this can be enjoyed for many more weeks. It can be worthwhile, if you start one right at the beginning of spring, to plant a succession of seeds, for instance, each month right up till autumn. These seeds also will succeed better if soaked first. They will not need as long as those of the sweet peas, twenty-four hours should do, and soil need not be as rich. Nip dead blooms off each day or so to prolong flowering.

Although it lacks the breathtaking blue shade, moonflower is just as exciting in a different way. There is still the rapid growth, but the joy of these white flowers comes in the evening, when one can watch the slow unfolding of the umbrellalike buds from the neatly furled stage to the final glory of the beautiful round flower. In some areas there will be a distinct perfume, which seems to belong to only this member of the big group of convolvulaceous plants, but this is not always present. There are other colors and varieties available in this family of annual climbers, but none equal these two. *Ipomoea* "Heavenly Blue" and moonflower can be grown in the same pot, as they require very little root room. This will give you a "day-and-night" effect. For a short time in early morning they will be in flower together, but only until moonflower goes to bed for the day.

CHAPTER SIXTEEN

Plants for Hanging Baskets

Whether or not you will be able to grow hanging basket plants successfully on your balcony will be largely determined by the amount of wind to which it is subjected. This will also govern the types of plants you can grow. Some of the hardier ones will survive even when being spun around and around for much of the day. I have seen coleuses grow successfully under these conditions. They are extremely hardy, grow quickly from cuttings and if you can get an assortment of colors and leaf forms, they will be decorative for many weeks. Good watering is essential, as it is for all basket-grown plants.

When you start your basket, put one of the several kinds of water-retaining plastic foam preparations in with the potting soil. If your garden shop does not carry any of these, go to a department store and get a packet of the plastic foam filling that is sold for stuffing cushions. This will serve admirably. It will greatly help to keep the roots damp. In hot weather you will still need to water quite often. There are some useful plastic waterers with long curved spouts that save one from the business of having to climb up on chairs if the plants are very high. Also some of the spray atomizers available are fitted with such long nozzles. Look around for these handy items in garden stores and department stores.

Geraniums, accustomed to growing in windy window-boxes for centuries, will not complain about hanging basket conditions, but they do ask for some sun. There are many kinds to choose from; compact growers and the trailing varieties are available. If you do have a sunny location, think also of petunias, which can be very colorful. There are many new varieties. The cascade types, which will give gay color and perfume for many weeks in summer, are especially suitable for baskets. Beautiful effects can be created using either all one color, an assortment or just red and white. Also, you can achieve lovely effects by combining petunias with other flowers such as pansies, violas, ageratum, lobelia, marigolds and geraniums.

Ball-type Baskets

Sometimes several types of flowers can be combined to make a "ball" effect by using wire baskets lined with sphagnum moss (sometimes called "florists' moss") and then inserting the plants between the wires at the sides of the baskets as well as planting them on the top. The moss lining must be about 1-inch (3-cm) thick to retain both moisture and soil, and it also should be about 1 inch (3 cm) higher than the soil on the top.

The soil used must be as lightweight as possible, because these baskets, being necessarily large, will be quite heavy when wet. You need a basket at least 12 inches (30 cm) and preferably 14 inches (35 cm) in diameter. Heavy feeding is also essential because much space is occupied by the moss, which does not provide nourishment. A good general fertilizer should be given every two weeks, or alternatively add liquid fertilizer to water each day.

You can make smaller ball-type baskets by using a smaller basket and following the same procedure with smaller plants such as alyssum, lobelia or violas. I once saw a beautiful effect on a patio where these hanging "balls" consisted of alternating white and purple alyssum, and edging the patio beneath them were matching pots of the same alternating colors. Of course you can use ivy or any of the hardier evergreens in the same way. These would last longer than the annual flowers, which also need more attention in the matter of removing the spent flowers.

Generally speaking, plastic baskets with clip-on saucers are much easier to use than the wire ones, although they will not, of course, do for the special effects just described. They are easier to position than the wire ones, which lack anything to catch drips, unless of course you are able to hang them above a good-sized plant, which can take care of the surplus water. These and wire baskets both come in the half-round shapes that are very good for hanging flat on a wall.

Fuchsias

For the shaded balconies where wind is not too great a problem, nothing is lovelier for baskets than the gracefully drooping fuchsias. There are so many varieties that I will not attempt to enumerate them here. Some are more pendulous than others, and most garden shops will carry stocks of all types. If you buy those already planted in baskets you can be sure of their suitability, but any of those with soft, pendulous-looking stems will be fine. Fuchsias are lovely in half-baskets against the wall too.

Fuchsias.

If you know of a good potter, it could be worth while getting some half-round planters made, into which pots could be fitted. Some-times these can be found in garden shops, and if you can find one of the type copied from the classical Italian designs these can be very decorative, especially when filled with ivy as they often are in Italian gardens.

Shade-loving Plants

Primulas and cinerarias make attractive basket plants for shaded balconies, as do the many colors of impatiens ("busy Lizzie"), that hardy little warrior now being produced in attractive variegated forms. The trailing campanulas are lovely too, and have the advan-tage of being perennial, as do the hardier types of fern and the old reliable wandering Jew (or "weary Willie") in variegated forms. The donkey's tail sedum, with its long, ropelike "tails" often growing up to 1 yard in length, is very decorative and hardy, tolerating either shade or almost full sun in most areas. There is also a small-leafed plant that I really love, Ceropegia *woodii* (or "hearts entwined," to give it its more romantic popular name, derived from its prettily speckled heart-shaped leaves). The flowers are not exciting, but the long pendulous stems with all their little hearts are very appealing. This plant prefers shade but it will take some sun also.

Another flowering plant that also likes shade is *Zygocactus truncatus,* or Christmas cactus, which can be found in many attrac-tive colors. It must be kept quite moist except during its resting pe-riod just after flowering, when watering should be reduced. Also, give less water when buds are forming, as overwatering at this time could cause them to drop. This plant needs a fairly coarse compost or leaf mold.

Schizanthus

No list of hanging basket suggestions should conclude without men-tion of the lovely *Schizanthus* ("poor man's orchid"). Beautiful either in pots or baskets, the masses of tiny orchidlike flowers come in a lovely range of colors. This is an annual that needs a protected loca-tion because of its brittle leaves and stems. For partly enclosed balconies it is ideal and can be grown in many climates. It can be raised from seed, sown uncovered in a dark cool place. If this is a problem, it may be possible to get seedlings or small potted plants. It is worth searching for.

Vines

Many of the vines suggested in chapter 15 on climbing plants will grow well in baskets. Some of the fast-growing ones will need to be pruned, or to have their long stems looped back into the basket. This is a good way of thickening your planting, as many of these vines, such as the hoyas, ceropegias and philodendrons, have aerial roots that will provide new plants when tucked back into the soil. These can be removed later if you want to start additional plants.

Hoya Bella

Unlike its larger relatives, *Hoya Bella* is small and does not grow upward, but prefers to hang down, making it an ideal hanging basket subject. The stems are very soft and the flowers similar to other hoyas in form and fragrance, but these, and the leaves, are much smaller. Hoya is often known as "wax plant" for its unusually wax-like texture. It likes a rich soil, but will not need frequent repotting; in fact, this should only be done when absolutely necessary as the roots tend to resent disturbance.

Bougainvilleas

Where there is enough sun, bougainvilleas will make excellent hanging basket plants. Be sure to get the softer-stemmed varieties. They will tolerate a good deal of wind and will also do well if the baskets are hung from a trellis on

Azaleas and trailing striptocarpus.

a sunny wall. Even if you do not have half-baskets, it is a simple matter to adjust the wires of the round plastic baskets to let them hang against a wall.

Lobelias and Petunias

Smaller plants such as lobelias and the cascade form of petunias can also be used in pots suspended in wire rings, which can also be hooked into a trellis. A trough filled with plants just beneath this trellis will take care of the drips in these cases. If you are not able to find a trough with a matching tray, get one made by the nearest sheet-metal worker, but be sure it is galvanized.

CHAPTER SEVENTEEN

Bonsai for Balconies and Terraces

Bonsai can be grown quite successfully on balconies, even those exposed to a good deal of wind, if the right varieties are chosen. In fact, some of the pines, especially those most prized in the Japanese connoisseurs' collections, have come from the high mountains where strong winds were originally responsible for their wonderful, gnarled shapes.

No amount of careful wiring in nurseries can ever equal the shapes thus created. That is why the more treasured and certainly the most expensive of these marvelous little trees are those originally carefully dug up in the high mountains, their long, long roots being painstakingly wrapped and then planted in the ground in a specialist nursery. The trees live at the nursery for a period of years during which their roots are periodically shortened back, a little at a time, until they are finally ready to be potted in the incredibly small, shallow containers in which they are finally sold. And if they fall into the right hands, they will continue to live for many years, possibly centuries.

Pines and Junipers

Most of the pines grown as bonsai are the Japanese black pine *(Pinus thunbergii)*, red pine *(P. densiflora)* and five-needled pine *(P. pentaphylla)*. There are also several varieties of juniper that are used in the same way.

Most of us must be content to buy our pines or junipers from a western nursery where they are now becoming more readily available, either already trained or in the form of young seedlings. The red and black pines will grow quickly. The five-needle type is much slower, and seedlings take many years to reach a reasonable size. Space here does not permit a detailed description of the cultivation of these pines and junipers.

Black pine bonsai.

Holly

Holly is a freely seeding plant that makes very attractive bonsai with or without its lovely berries. A search beneath mature bushes will nearly always turn up good little seedlings, the older ones possibly already well on the way to having a good branching form. Another lovely plant with leaves very similar to a miniature variegated holly, but with wonderfully fragrant flowers, is *Osmanthus aquifolium,* which is easily trained into lovely forms. Its relative, *Osmanthus fragrans,* has the most beautifully apricot-scented flowers. They are quite insignificant, but will scent the air all around. I have grown it as a bonsai, but it is not so adaptable as *O. aquifolium,* as its leaves and stems are very stiff. It grows readily from cuttings in cooler climates, and this gives you a good chance of shaping the little plants from infancy. It is much faster-growing than *O. aquifolium,* but they are both treasures and not nearly as well known in some regions as they deserve to be. *O. fragrans* is seen quite often in Japanese gardens.

Rosemary

Another plant that few people would think of growing as a bonsai but that can be most satisfactory is rosemary. Either the upright or the prostrate form will train remarkably well. Being fairly fast-growing, frequent clipping is needed, and the clippings are great for cooking. Rosemary is marvelous in soups, stews, casseroles and finely-chopped in toasted sandwiches. (In fact, when you discover how useful this plant is, you will probably need at least two plants.)

Cherry Banyan

One tree that is also ideal for bonsai in the charming little cherry banyan, or mistletoe banyan *(Ficus diversifolia).* A much slower grower, this little tree is covered, even from infancy, in attractive little green, white and sometimes red berries. It has small rounded leaves, grows easily from cuttings and lends itself to a variety of shapes.

Wind

I was lucky enough to attend a course of lessons at Yuji Yoshimura's nursery in Tokyo many years ago, and it was in this nursery that I saw a great way to keep plants from blowing over on windy balconies. This was to pass wire at each end of the rectangular pots, right over the soil, and then to secure these wires to the shelf on which the plants stood. This was for a number of plants that were mounted upon platforms set on the tops of posts dotted about the nursery, presumably to highlight the choicest specimens.

When growing bonsai, make a point of collecting a number of heavy decorative waterworn or weathered stones. These will not only add greatly to the decorative effect of your plants, but will also serve to help anchor them against strong winds and to conserve moisture, especially in the case of the very shallow containers so frequently used and which dry out so quickly. There are a great many ways to combine the stones as part of the actual planting, by setting the plants on top of them, or in any small hollows, with the roots going down the sides into the soil beneath. This is particularly effective with the small figs *(Ficus spp.),* which have such ornamental roots, often as important as the branches and the foliage. The pines already mentioned also lend themselves to this type of planting. They acquire a look of greater age when the roots are thus seen on the surface. You must follow instructions in doing these plantings so that there are enough roots in the soil to maintain a healthy plant, and most important, great care must be taken in keeping these plants well watered so that the exposed roots will not dry out too much.

Other plants that will stand up to heavy wind are the pyracanthas (formerly classified as *Cratraegus*) and the smaller forms of cotoneaster, all of which have beautiful berries, are fast-growing and respond very well to shaping. Then there are the flowering cherries, the *Prunus* genus, so beloved of the Japanese, and the beautiful little crab-apples. Many other fruiting trees are also available. The big citrus family with its beautiful small forms—the charming little calomondin orange, the chinoti, the various kumquats, pears, quinces, pomegranates and even the normal valencia orange and lemons—can be dwarfed if grafted onto small-growing stocks. The list is long, and the choice can be agonizing, especially when space is limited.

Space

So, one solution is to set about seeing how many can be accommodated in the space available. If there is a good area of wall, try a sort of "bookshelf" arrangement, with the lower shelves wider than the higher ones so that the shelves above (if made of wood) will not keep too much light away from the bottom row of plants. If the shelves are made of glass, this problem will not arise, assuming that the plants are staggered in such a way that none is directly above another. Fortunately, there are many types of stands available these days. If you are fortunate enough to have a post on your balcony, you can put a series of rounded shelves around it. Some furniture stores stock wrought-iron "baker's racks," with a series of shelves that would accommodate many plants.

It is a good idea to concentrate on keeping the plants small in order to have more variety. The big spreading types are best for open gardens where they can be seen to better advantage anyway. We who have only a little area must "scale down."

Aspect

All of the varieties already enumerated, with the exception of the banyans, must have a sunny aspect. This applies to most flowering and fruiting trees, but it is especially so for most "needled" evergreens. If deprived of sun the shoots will tend to grow out weak and "leggy," which will not contribute to the sturdy, compact form that is essential of all bonsai.

There are many varieties, however, that will thrive in partial, or even complete, shade. These include the many varieties of the lovely maples, azaleas, miniature rhododendrons, cycads, bamboos and, perhaps the most

Azaleas are well-adapted to becoming bonsai.

adaptable of all, the several smaller forms of the large *Ficus* genus. My little 12-inch high (30-cm) specimen of the same member of this genus has full-grown siblings that are so huge they've become one of the "sights" on several of the Hawaiian Islands and in many other tropical regions. These magnificent giants cover enormous areas of ground, sending down aerial roots that, when they reach the ground, become trees themselves. In a few years there is a large grove, all attached to the original parent tree. The wonderful gnarled trunks of these trees are reproduced in bonsai forms, and as this takes place at a relatively early age, one certainly does not have to wait years and years to grow a quite ancient-looking specimen of this Bengal banyan *(Ficus benghalensis).*

Choice of suitable plants will depend entirely on your climate (see chapter 1 for information). A careful look around the local nurseries

Camellia treated as bonsai.

will not only give an idea of what subjects do well in your area, but may also reveal some that are suitable for cutting down into bonsai.

In the warmer climates it is not difficult to buy small plants of this ficus in 4-inch (100-mm) pots, which will already have begun to show signs of a fairly heavy trunk. A similar fig that I grew in Sydney, *F. rubiginosa,* had the same characteristics, and even a six- or seven-year-old seedling would already have quite a bulbous trunk. It seems that the latter variety grows better in cooler climates than does *F. benghalensis.* With both of these, it is best to push them along fairly quickly in not-too-small pots for the first few years so that they make good branch and leaf growth, which can be pruned often to create a bushy top. They are both extremely hardy, growing either in sun, semi-shade or even complete shade. This gives them the very valuable advantage of being suitable for year-round indoor culture, something to which only a few other bonsai will submit. Most of the other species of the *Ficus* genus have this endearing trait. There are actually more plants suitable for bonsai available to cold-climate gardeners than in the tropical areas. This is good, because in the long winters when there are few flowers and many trees are bare, a collection of bonsai can provide a great amount of interest and decoration. Even in cases of deciduous varieties, their shapes are attractive year-round. Camellias, for one, really come into their own in winter, and many varieties are suitable for bonsai. Oddly enough the best I have seen were *C. sasanqua* types, and although I have stated in chapter 13 on camellias that I do not recommend the *sasanquas* for larger balcony plants, when well pruned as bonsai, the prostrate form can be very attractive. There are several smaller types also, and they have the added bonus of having glossy evergreen leaves, which are always decorative.

Flowering Trees

Among the flowering plants suitable for bonsai, try bougainvilleas for hot climates and azaleas for cooler climates. You should have good luck with these. Japanese nursery workers have had wonderful results with their Satsuki azaleas. The small-growing "Gumpo" types, now becoming more available, are ideal for growing as bonsai where space is limited. In some areas they will have a fairly long flowering period, but it must be remembered that few azaleas are particularly interesting when not in flower unless they are ancient bonsai, whose branch formation is beautiful in itself.

An azalea the author trained as bonsai.

There are many lovely varieties of *Prunus spp.,* cherry and other deciduous trees to which this will also apply, and, if space is very limited, it might be best to pass these up in favor of the evergreens or plants such as the lovely *Pieris japonica* (formerly *Andromeda*) with its lovely lily-of-the-valley-like racemes of white or pink bells, which stay in bloom for a long time. The leaves of this plant remain throughout the year, and the new spring growth is a beautiful pink; it is so decorative that many Japanese gardens feature the leaves rather than the flowers. This lovely plant, however, is only for the cold or cooler climates.

Fast-Growing Trees

Some plants can be grown from cuttings quickly and manage to look reasonably mature in a few years. Outstanding among these is the willow. Any of the several varieties are suitable. If a thick branch is cut in late winter or early spring, left in water until a good root system is formed, then potted in an attractive Chinese or Japanese pot, you will soon have the interesting task of cutting and shaping branches to make a compact form before allowing them to hang in their inimitably graceful way when the plant is placed on a high stand or shelf. Do not be disappointed if your cuttings die when first potted. They sometimes do, so have several on hand. (You can always give the surplus away.) Once they are established, growth will be so rapid (if you have the right conditions) that both roots and top growth will need pruning twice a year. At least a third of the roots can be safely cut away. Replant in good rich soil. Willows like plenty of water, and the pots can even stand in saucers of water.

Quick results can also be had from fast-growing seedlings. Possibly the most satisfactory of these are the lovely Japanese maples. Large trees nearly always have a crop of seedlings beneath them, and these, when lifted and potted in good soil, will grow very rapidly and are very amenable to shaping. In areas where growth is rapid, some wiring of the trunks will be needed, but the wire must not be left on too long. Check it frequently lest it cut into the bark. Scars result if left this way, and they will never grow out. If necessary, loosen the wires every few months. You can make a small group planting of these little maples in a wide shallow container. They look very attractive when grouped toward one end of rectangular Japanese bonsai pots. There is often a problem in getting the right size saucers for these pots, but either a small tray or those shallow plastic or Styrofoam trays on which fruits, vegetables and cuts of meat are sold in the supermarkets serve very well. They are surprisingly strong, especially if painted, top and bottom. Black looks best, shows fewer marks and fits in with the Japanese theme.

Pine seedlings are certainly worth trying if you happen to be in an area where they grow well (usually cold or moderately cool regions). Sometimes these can be difficult to lift, as they put down long tap roots, and it is just as simple to raise them from seed. When we lived in the cold mountains, I used to pick up cones that had fallen from the varieties of pine that I liked best, waiting until they had just begun to open. The seeds fall out easily when you knock the cones together. They will usually come up quickly; some types take longer, but wait for them.

Plant the seeds in soil containing at least some portion of soil from where the parent tree is growing; this will contain a useful fungus called mycorrhiza, which has a beneficial effect on the roots of pines. When the time comes to repot any of your pines, remember again to get some soil from beneath healthy pines, even if it needs to be combined with a richer sandy mix sold especially for bonsai. When the time comes to pot these little pines on, it is also best to shorten the long tap root that the seedlings will have made; otherwise, it will grow around and around their next pot. Also they should be encouraged to form side roots. Take off about one third. Some varieties of pine will, like the *Ficus,* form quite thick trunks at an early age, making them perfect for bonsai.

Remember that pines will not be happy indoors. If you want to take your pet bonsai into the house for a time, do not keep it there too long. Give it a sunny position.

Within the larger, fast-growing varieties, we have a treasure in the graceful, pendulous weeping fig or Benjamin banyan *(Ficus benjamina),* which, like its cousin from Bengal, grows into a very large spreading tree but can also be tamed into a most attractive indoor or balcony specimen. It is extremely hardy, very decorative and adapts perfectly to being kept indoors for apparently unlimited periods, provided that its small requirements of reasonable amounts of light, air and water are met.

F. benjamina's graceful pendulous habit of growth makes it suitable for many more purposes than those of its heavier-leafed cousins, *F. decora* and *F. elastica*. Rate of growth depends entirely on climate. In Hawaii, it reaches 6 feet (2 m) in just a few years, but in colder climates it grows more slowly and is, consequently, more expensive. Whether large or small, it is a treasure. If grown outdoors it will take sun, but it appears to be happier in shade or semishade. This tree has now become as fashionable as was *F. decora* a few years ago, and is therefore not always easy to get. It is worthwhile looking around for small potted seedlings or trying some cuttings if you have a friend with a large tree. It would have to be treated as one of your larger bonsai because of its open habit of growth, but I believe it could be kept at around 18 inches (45 cm) high for quite a time.

The "Tortured Tree" Myth

Of course, anyone who grows bonsai will sooner or later (and often quite frequently) encounter friends who will shudder at the "cruelties" inflicted on these "poor little tortured trees!" Often, the shudderer is one who regularly prunes his hedges and trees and mows his lawns without any thought of being cruel. It is useless to point out that besides the fact that one could hardly accommodate a 45-foot (15-m) pine or maple on one's balcony, these trees are neither dwarfed, starved or stunted. Through careful root and branch pruning and pinching, they are controlled, but not thwarted. The accusation that their small size is the result of neglect and starvation is the direct opposite of the truth. They must have meticulous, regular and, above all, loving care to survive.

As one grower put it, "You certainly get more mileage as a conversation-promoter, out of one bonsai than you would from three dozen ordinary pot plants. I recommend it to anyone who wants an easy way to get an animated argument going!" The same writer said of her first experience of root pruning, "I found the whole operation nerve-racking, rather like cutting your first baby's fingernails for the first time You I now it has to be done, but wonder how you're going to feel if ..." I think we must have all had the same misgivings, but one grows bolder with practice, and in no time at all we are snipping and shearing away (sometimes with too much gusto).

"Instant" Bonsai

When the bonsai bug first bit me, I haunted the older nurseries, and sometimes the smaller one-person kind where neglected plants had been thrust into the background, having not been regarded as good enough for seasonal repotting. These areas can be goldmines, and often sell at bargain prices. You will enjoy the challenge of finding well-advanced trees (usually in oversized old tins), taking them home, and pruning back roots and branches. It may take a few seasons to achieve perfection in some cases; in many other cases near-perfection is assured as soon as the pruning process is completed.

This is the perfect solution for the gardener who is not willing to wait for the maturing of seedlings and cuttings, and certainly this "instant-bonsai" method can be enormously rewarding. One must be prepared to search diligently, however, for competition is great these days with so many bonsai addicts always on the prowl. Even when fairly large branches have to be cut back, it is possible to disguise these cuts by carefully filing down the stubs. After a time they will blend into the color of the rest of the trunk. It may be advisable to do the root pruning in installments at one-year intervals. Remember that when you prune roots you must also cut off a corresponding amount of the top growth.

A Note on Root Pruning

It must be remembered that no more than one third of a plant's roots should be removed at one time. Also remember that frequency of root pruning varies with different trees. For instance, members of the pine family (and most needled trees) should only be root pruned every three to five years, whereas those tough characters, the willows and the wisterias, will probably need it every six months in areas where they grow rapidly. It is difficult to lay down definite rules in the light of the great many varieties of plants now being grown as bonsai, and also of the greatly varying conditions in different climates.

Get a good book on bonsai, for there is much to be learned about this fascinating art. There are now many excellent books on the subject of bonsai, perhaps the most authoritative being *Miniature Trees and Landscapes* by Yuji Yoshimura and Giovanna Halford. But keep in mind that the best books will probably be written in Japan and will almost certainly deal with conditions in that country (possibly even just one area of it). You will be well advised to more or less "play it by ear" if yours is a different climate. As with any form of gardening, only careful study of one's own conditions and knowledge gained by experience will ensure any degree of success. And while you are gaining this invaluable "know-how," you will be experiencing the most rewarding (even if often frustrating) of all the pastimes that anyone could hope to enjoy.

CHAPTER EIGHTEEN

Vegetables in Containers

The staggering rise in food prices all over the world and the increased use of agricultural chemicals has brought about a tremendous interest in vegetable growing, and even apartment dwellers are experimenting with the smaller-growing items, often with surprising success. I am one of these experimenters, and I would strongly recommend this most interesting and rewarding form of balcony gardening to anyone with even just a few feet of available space. Vegetable growing on your balcony or patio can be one of the most rewarding summer activities. It is ever so lovely to treat guests to a salad with ingredients from your balcony.

Snowpeas.

Sun

There is just one "must," however, and this is sunshine. Even a few hours of sun will suffice, preferably morning sun, but this is not essential. Midday or afternoon is better than none, especially if reflected heat can be given from warm walls. It will help too, to place pots close to a wall in order to have as much protection against wind, which presents the biggest problem to most balcony gardeners.

Wind

Sometimes a glass, Perspex or wire mesh shelter can be erected to help break the force of destructive winds. This need not be high enough to cause concern as to the regulations governing most apartment or unit buildings; sometimes a fly-screen door laid on its side against the balcony railing will break the main force without excluding too much of the all-important sun.

If you are at ground level, this problem will not be nearly so acute. You might even be able to try creating a screen of climbing beans. I recently saw a charming screen that featured "Scarlet Runner," a variety with the extra bonus of red flowers. The beans were planted in long troughs from which heavy string was stretched to a board that edged the balcony ceiling above. The same idea can be used against a wall if there is a danger of the "bean screen" excluding too much light from the rest of the balcony. This can be easily controlled by the spacing of the beans at planting time. In either case, there is room for other low-growing items in front of the beans. Lettuces are good here as they, like beans, give quick results.

If this arrangement does not fit in with the existing scheme, or if there is not a suitable board to which to nail the strings, it can be worthwhile trying the beans in big round or square pots with a tall wire-netting cylinder in the center, or a tripod made from stakes. Bush or dwarf beans will also do quite well. Pots can be mounted on casters so that they can be moved to catch the most sun. Many stores now sell various sized wood platforms fitted with casters for easy removal of plants, or it may be cheaper to make such platforms at home. (They are handy for moving house plants as well.)

Soil

For smaller-sized pots, which can still be quite heavy to lift if soil is on the heavy side, use a mixture containing a good proportion of vermiculite, which is feather light but still very good for retention of moisture and also for good drainage. Many ready-to-use potting mixtures contain a good deal of this medium. These pot plant mixtures, although more expensive than ordinary garden soil, are usually worth the extra cost. They are easy to handle, and the good brands will have well-balanced proportions and will be sterilized. Most have some fertilizer added, but this will need to be supplemented, in most cases, when the vegetables get under way. I still believe the best fertilizer is animal manure, even though this may present some problems in confined areas, but poultry manure can usually be bought in small packages. It must be used sparingly if plants and pots are small. Failing this, any general garden fertilizer can be used, with perhaps the addition of some liquid fertilizer when plants come into flower.

Watering

It must always be remembered that vegetables grown in containers will require watering more regularly than those in the ground. Unless the weather is cloudy or wet, they will almost certainly need water every day. Feeding must be attended to at regular intervals also, using either a general fertilizer or, in the case of tomatoes, one of the special types of tomato food. Quantities shown on the package should be halved for any plants grown in pots.

Pest and Disease Protection

Trouble from pests or disease will vary with climate and season. There are special tomato and vegetable dusts. If you find it necessary to use a general insecticide, take care that you do not use any of the poisonous sprays too close to harvesting time. Usually those containing pyrethrum are safest for vegetable crops. (See also chapter 20 on pests.)

Space

A number of people prefer to grow their vegetables in troughs and tubs even though they have garden space. They maintain that care is much easier when plants are in containers; certainly one does not have to stoop so far, and weeding is far easier. Also I know people who have grown tomatoes by both methods and assert that those grown in containers are superior and less trouble. One man in California has a small area in his garden where he grows all his vegetables in a series of redwood troughs arranged very interestingly in a series of built-up tiers. These redwood troughs can be made by hand or purchased from a number of garden supply sources. And even if you do not plan on such a large-scale arrangement as this, one or two make a decorative edging for a terrace or on either side of a path. Discarded round washing-machine bowls and half casks can be used very effectively also.

The balcony gardener usually has to be content with smaller containers, for, even where space may permit, there is always the difficult problem of finding a drip tray to catch water drainage. Troughs present a problem in such cases unless one is lucky enough to have a balcony with a drainage gutter. On the whole it is usually simpler to have a series of large plastic pots with either plastic or metal saucers beneath. For the larger size for which saucers are hard to find, inexpensive metal or plastic drink trays will serve very well. If there is a sunny wall that can carry a section of trellis, some climbing plants can still be planted in these pots at its base.

Tomatoes

The number of vegetables suitable for container growing is very large. I have even seen corn growing in the large tubs, but a good deal of space is needed for this. Probably the ideal plant for container growing is the tomato in its various forms. While the large-fruiting kinds can be used, generally speaking, the smaller types are easier to manage and give a very good yield. I have found that the very small cherry tomato, also known as "Tiny Tim," does extremely well and produces clusters of fruit very early in its life.

Tomatoes.

Also small, though larger than the cherry-sized one, with fruit about ³/₄- to 1-inch (2- to 3-cm) wide is "Small Fry," which produces its fruit also in clusters of six to ten. "Small Fry" will grow quite decoratively in hanging baskets. Actually, these small tomatoes can be grown on a sunny windowsill, but they must be assured of good light and plenty of sun. Sown in autumn, they will produce throughout the winter in temperate climates, especially if the room in which they are grown is centrally heated. Slightly larger are "Pixie" and "Patio Hybrid" with fruit 1 to 2 inches (3 to 5 cm) in diameter, also borne in clusters. "Pixie" grows about 18 inches (45 cm) high and "Patio Hybrid" and "Small Fry" are somewhat taller. "Tiny Tim" averages about 12 inches (30 cm). The last, being the smallest, can be grown in a 6-inch (15-cm) pot, but the others will do best in a 12-inch (30-cm) container. Support will be needed in all cases, and this can take the form of one or more stakes or a cylinder of chicken wire surrounding each plant. A small trellis can be used as well.

Tomatoes are always popular. I suggest you buy starter plants from your nursery, department store or the grocery store. Determinate tomatoes (which include dwarf varieties suitable for container growing) are compact, bushy varieties that produce all of their fruit over a short period, then stop growing. These varieties are best for short growing seasons and are also convenient for gardeners who want to preserve tomatoes.

Peppers

Peppers of all kinds make great container vegetables. Remember that peppers are tropical plants
that need a constantly moist atmosphere, daytime
tempertures between 70 and 80°F and nighttime
temperatures between 60 and 70°F. Peppers will
not bloom or set fruit and will even drop flowers
and immature fruit if exposed to hot, dry or cold
conditions.

Peppers.

Again, I recommend buying your starter
plants rather than growing from seed. If you buy
transplants, do not buy plants already in bloom or
bearing small fruits. Newly planted peppers need several weeks
to establish roots; diverting a young plant's energy to producing
fruit will result in a permanently stunted plant by midseason.

Beans

Beans can be fun in any tight environemnt, especially any of the
"pole" beans. One friend tied strings from her balcony railing to
the ceiling. The beans climbed the string, mak-
ing a lovely trellis effect. But even more fun
was when her upstairs neighbor continued
the strings up to his ceilings and his upstairs neighbor followed suit. All three
tenants enjoyed the shade from the climbing beans (plus the wonder harvest).

When planting beans, remember they
are tender annuals. They need warm
weather to grow well and will not tolerate even a light frost. Do not plant them
too early, because seeds may rot in cold,
wet soil.

To improve the plants' ability to fix nitrogen in the soil, treat seeds with a legume

String Beans.

inoculent powder (available from mail-order companies and garden centers) before planting.

Pole beans produce their crop more slowly than bush beans, but they bear more heavily and over a longer period of time. Baby lima beans bear ealrier than large varieties. Supports for pole beans should be in place before seeds are planted. Remember beans do not transplant well, so plant them where you want them and leave them there.

Eggplant

Many of my friends have experimented with more "exotic" balcony vegetables. Small-fruited and dwarf varieties of eggplant make good container plants. Again, buying your starter plants is easier than trying to start plants inside. Long-season varieties grow best in areas where summers are hot and fall weather is mild. Elsewhere, plant the early variet-ies. When hardening off eggplant prior to trans-planting, do not expose the seedlings to cold or to water withdrawal as you would for other types of transplants. Eggplant seedlings exposed to cold may fail to flower or set fruit.

Eggplant.

Squash

Squash plants make lovely additions to a balcony. The plant is bushy. Definitely stick to the smaller varieties, avoiding the vining squash varieties. All squash plants are very tender and grow best in warm temperatures averaging 50° to 70°F. In cooler climates, a black plastic container will provide much needed warmth to the roots. All squashes are heavy feeders, so a soil rich in organic matter and nutrients is essential for maximum yields.

Squash.

As to which vegetables to grow, the variety is enormous. If your plot is very small it would be worth searching for some of the "mini"-type vegetables, now being sold for smaller areas. These are small replicas of normal varieties specially hybridized for present-day requirements. If not available, send for some mail-order seed catalogs. Do not mistake small-fruiting varieties that grow on normal-sized plants for these miniatures. The latter are true midgets, both fruit and plants.

CHAPTER NINETEEN

Herbs

It should be no problem to grow all the herbs you want to grow on your balcony. Most of them can be kept small enough to fit around the edges of larger tubs or pots, and an edging of parsley, chives or basil looks quite attractive and saves space. Oregano is nice and compact for growing with other plants, and so are the various kinds of thyme.

An herb rack.

Basil

Basil is a very useful herb, as it is the tallest of these to plant beneath trees that have lost their leaves or have become a little "leggy," and it

111

is an accommodating plant and can easily be kept low if you do not need this type of camouflage. I find it enormously useful for a range of recipes and always keep a few leaves in a jar of oil and vinegar salad dressing. It gives a very pleasant flavor, is good finely chopped in the salad itself and is especially harmonious with tomatoes. When you have a good crop it can be dried for winter use, as can most herbs. It is very easily raised from seed scattered where it is to grow. This can be done also with parsley. If you have difficulty growing basil from seed it is always possible to find small plants of this ever-popular plant.

Chives

Chives are always useful, and there are usually several varieties to be had, so why not have an assortment? Do not despair if your chives eventually die away. This is normal and seasonal, and they will probably reappear next spring.

Mint

If you are just wild about mint, there are many varieties that work well on balconies, but be careful. Mint is best kept in a pot to itself, as you will realize if you have had it romp all over garden beds and tried to track the long tenacious roots. Its growth is not so rampant in a pot, but it is nevertheless inclined to take possession and choke other plants. For this reason mint should not be included in any container of mixed herbs.

Mint.

Lemon Balm

Lemon balm is a delightful herb for any balcony. Seeds need light to germinate, and the plants love full sun to partial shade. Press seeds

lightly into the soil, but do not cover with soil. To root cuttings, remove the lower leaves and insert them into soil from one-third to
one-half their length. Lemon balm is actually a hardy perennial that
needs moist soil but is prone to powdery mildew,
so be careful of overcrowding.

Borage

Borage is an attractive herb, with its pretty
blue flowers. Like basil, it is an annual but is
easily raised from seed each year. The leaves,
with their cucumber-like taste, are a very
pleasant addition to fruit salad or punch. The
flowers can be effectively crystallized, but they
also make a very pretty decoration on sweets and
in drinks when used fresh. Leaves are used in
many ways for cooking and chopped in salads.
The plant has an ancient reputation for im-
parting cheerfulness and courage, not to
mention a number of other healing attributes.
It is pretty enough to be grown by itself, but
could share a pot or tub with tall plants or
trees. Both the leaves and flowers of borage can be infused for an herbal tea.

Comfrey

Borage.

Comfrey, a larger relative of borage, has
been used since medieval times to heal a number of ailments, even
having been given the name of "knit-bone" at one time because of its
ability to speed the healing of broken bones. Modern-day health food
enthusiasts are very keen on it. If you can find a copy of *Culpepers
Complete Herbal,* written originally in the early seventeenth century
and reprinted by W. Foulsham of London, it provides very enter-
taining reading about this and many other herbs. Comfrey's culinary
value is not great as the leaves are somewhat tough with prickly hairs
and little taste, but much has been said of its curative powers. It can

be grown in a large pot, but it is a very strong grower and should not be combined with other plants. Its strong roots (also of great medicinal value) need a pot to themselves. It has been said that comfrey leaves are delicious when dipped in batter and then fried in hot oil.

Comfrey.

Bay Tree

A "must" even in your little garden is a bay tree. Bay trees will grow slowly for many years in pots and are best kept in a pot by themselves. They can be gradually trained into the popular European round or cone shape as you use the aromatic leaves. The older leaves should be cut first. Although they are sold dried, fresh from the plant, they are wonderful for all soups, casseroles and roasts. They are happier in cold than in hot climates, growth being slower in the latter case, but even a small plant will be sufficient for most needs.

Strawberry Pot

If you do not have any suitable large containers in which to grow your herbs with larger plants, the best way to plant them is in one of the old-fashioned strawberry pots that are now being used for almost everything except strawberries. These tall pots take up minimum space yet accommodate a surprising number of plants. They look very attractive too, especially if you take care to plant them so that the taller ones do not obscure the more compact varieties.

Plant carefully so that the plants do not sink beneath the pot's holes when the soil settles. Begin by putting a curved piece of crock or broken china over the drainage hole (curved side up) with a layer of gravel or some coarse fiber to ensure the very necessary drainage and to prevent soil penetrating down the sides of the crock. Then add just enough soil to reach the base of the lowest row of pockets. Water this soil before planting, and when it has settled plant the herbs from *inside* the pot, pulling the leaves gently to the outside. (If planted from the outside, the roots may suffer.) Now, cover the roots lightly, but before adding the next layer of soil, put a small piece of shade cloth over the opening of each "pocket" to prevent the soil from running out. Then proceed to fill up to the base of the next pocket, as before, letting the soil settle (even pressing it down gently) before planting each row. It can even be left and watered for several days before planting the herb in the top opening.

General purpose plant mix is the best for these plants, with some liquid plant food about once a month. Use the smaller growing herbs such as thyme, marjoram, lemon balm, chervil, oregano and chives for the side pockets. Parsley is good for the top section as it will not spread too much and keep the sun and light from the lower plants. Chives serve quite well here also. Dwarf, or prostrate, rosemary is good to plant in one of the lower pockets as it can then spread downward without crowding other plants. You will find this very useful.

The strawberry pot will need to be replanted in a year or so if the herbs have grown strongly. They can then be divided and repotted in new soil.

Cultivation

The way you pick the leaves of your herbs is rather important. Always take first the outside leaves of parsley and chervil. Cut basil sprigs from the top of the plants in order to keep them compact and prevent them from forming flowers and seeds, which will inhibit any further growth. At the end of the season, you can let one basil plant go to seed for next year, but in warm climates they can sometimes continue for quite a time without dying down if kept cut back. All the varieties of chives are best if continuously kept cut. This helps them to grow better.

Pesticides

It need hardly be emphasized that you must not use pesticides on plants growing in close proximity to herbs. In fact many of the herbs are themselves insect repellents. Basil is credited with not only going well with tomatoes in salads and cooked dishes, but with keeping insects and diseases away from the growing plants. It is also repellent to flies and mosquitoes. Oregano is said to keep beetles away from cucumbers, and tansy is said to discourage ants, aphids and flies. So tansy could be worth trying. Chives planted around roses are supposed to keep aphids away. Rue is said to have great insect repellent qualities, but as some of the other herbs refuse to grow in close contact with it, it could be best left out of small areas. Dried lavender, rosemary, tansy and lad's love are useful in keeping moths and silverfish away from clothes and books.

Herbs for a No-Salt Diet

Herbs are a great help in cooking if you are prescribed a no-salt diet. When my husband's doctor decreed, "No salt, either in cooking or on the table," it seemed a bleak prospect, but the basil, chives, bay leaves, rosemary and oregano came instantly, and most satisfactorily, to the rescue. We have long since ceased to miss the salt, and everything really tastes better than it did before. With the challenge of getting new flavors into our dishes, I have experimented with a number of herbs that were formerly only names to me. I highly recommend doing this.

Fortunately with the increasing interest in all kinds of herbs throughout the country, garden shops now carry quite good assortments of the better known types, and it is a good idea to visit an herb farm or specialist nursery to find out which is best suited to your climate and to get new varieties to try.

CHAPTER TWENTY

The Inevitable Pests

When I first became a balcony gardener, I recall remarking happily that at last I would be able to enjoy my plants and flowers without having to wage constant war against armies of chewing, sucking, crawling and constantly marauding insects that had kept me so busy in my large gardens. "They'll never come up as high as the fifteenth floor," I gloated confidently, carefully checking all newly bought plants for any signs of scale, thrip or red spider. Yet within a few weeks great masses of nasty green aphids were pushing and shoving one another for a foothold on every bud and flower of my bougainvilleas, and the horrible little brutes had even burrowed into the centers of the dendrobium orchids (right in the living room) while red spider mites were spoiling

Gypsy moth larvae.

118

the appearance of many of the leaves. Meanwhile the mealybugs had come to the party and started in on leaves and stems of the stephanotis, and an ugly brown scale covered the stems and leaves of my lovely jasmine. Yet another variety of scale had started in on the hibiscus, and the busy little ants, which had possibly been responsible for spreading so many of these pests, were scurrying about like efficient hosts making sure that everyone got their share of the goodies.

Little Black Ants

Did you know that little black ants are one of the gardener's greatest trials? They are certainly the hardest to eradicate because of their habit of making nests right down in the bottoms of pots, where it is impossible to reach them, and breeding there in a terribly prolific way. They apparently carry the eggs of aphids and mealybugs to all parts so that they can feed upon the sticky substance excreted by these insects. They actually "farm" them, as people farm cows, for their food supply.

So first, to get rid of these troublesome little farmers! There are many types of ant poisons to be found, some of which are temporarily effective. Ants can be sprayed with garden insecticides when they can be seen, but unfortunately, most of their feeding and wandering is done at night. It was when we noticed this that we were able to hit upon a weird home remedy that has proved more effective than any of the more sophisticated methods we have used.

Home Remedies

We had been dining one evening on the balcony, and had dropped a papaya (pawpaw) seed. A little later we noticed a huge number of ants crowding to get to this seed, and so it occurred to me that these might make quite a good trap. Accordingly we then spread out some newspaper with a goodly helping of the seeds in the center and awaited results. Sure enough, in less than half an hour the center of the paper was black with ants. Here is where speed must be combined with cunning. One must creep up very quietly, and quickly wrap up the paper tightly, wrap it again before enclosing it in a plastic bag and place the parcel in the garbage can. The wrapper-upper needs a partner for this operation, to hold a flashlight, which must be switched on at the last minute, as the ants usually feed in the dark. If you have sugar-eating ants, try mixing some sugar with borax and leave it in little heaps near the nests. This can be an effective poison.

Even though these methods are somewhat laborious, I always prefer any means of insect control to that of using pesticides that could be dangerous to birds and other friendly visitors.

It is perhaps in the field of pest control that the balcony gardener becomes most nostalgic for the garden hose of the down-to-earth days. Oh, for that beautiful strong spray of water which would dislodge aphids and mealy bugs so easily. I find that mealybugs will sometimes succumb to the strong spray of an atomizer, and for the more obstinate ones, I keep a second atomizer filled with soapy water. If you have not yet met mealybugs, they are white and fluffy. This also kills most types of aphids, but must not be left on the plants longer than fifteen or twenty minutes. Follow with a spraying of clear water, as the soap is too strong for most of the flowers or young leaf shoots to which these pests are attracted.

Some people use detergent for this, and it is easier to use than having to whip up soap, but it may be too strong, especially for more delicate flowers. This soapy water spray will also control several types of scale, but the more stubborn ones should be sprayed with white oil emulsion of which there are several brands to be had. Be sure to follow the label directions.

I also use the soapy water treatment for dunking long soft branches of bougainvillea and spraying orchids that are thickly clustered with aphids. Do this in a wide shallow basin. In this way the pests can be washed out of the deep trumpets in the centers of the orchids and under the curling petals. Leave it on for a short time to catch the stragglers, and then wash off with clear water.

If some escape there will be a fresh population in just a few days because the breeding rate of aphids is phenomenal. The eggs hatch in an incredibly short time. It becomes necessary to make sorties over several days, and then one may hope to have peace for a little while. How lucky are the cold-climate gardeners whose pests do at least have a dormant period in winter. In a year-round warm climate one has to be eternally vigilant.

For small plants where there are just a few hard-to-reach mealy bugs, many people prefer to use a cotton bud, cotton swab or a small piece of cotton wool wound around a toothpick or a longer thin stick dipped in alcohol or methylated spirits. This kills the pest on contact.

There are many other ways of dealing with pests without using dangerous pesticides. English scientist Mr. David Greenstock has developed a mixture of ground garlic, oil and water. He claims this will quickly kill greenfly, caterpillars, wireworms and snails, which plague English gardeners, while being harmless to ladybirds, birds and bees, which risk nothing worse than a bad case of halitosis. This is the recipe: Soak 90 grams of chopped garlic in 2 teaspoons of kerosene for 24 hours, then add 0.5 liter of water and mix well. Add a few milliliters of an oil-based soap to act as a spreading agent.

Another recipe, which is based on nicotine, should serve as a warning to persistent smokers as to how lethal this habit is. Boil 4 ounches (120 g) of nonfilter-tip cigarette ends in 4.75 quarts (4.5 l) of water for half an hour. Strain this through a nylon stocking. It will keep several weeks in a stoppered bottle. Diluted in four parts of water, it is said to kill even the most hardy of insects. You should not spray it on anything you are going to eat within a fortnight. Label the bottle "Poison," and be sure to wash your hands after using. Obviously this is a strong poison, and you should try the gentler methods first.

One balcony gardener I met stoutly maintains that he is able to keep down aphids by growing the strongly scented marigolds among his plants. This is worth trying if you do not mind the odor of marigolds. Nasturtiums and chives also have a reputation for repelling certain types of beetles. Chives are invaluable among your plants anyway, and a few bulbs can easily be tucked into the sides of pots holding larger plants.

Biological Insect Control

Constant research is being done in many countries on the question of biological insect control, and it is hoped that the day may come when more and more predator insects will be available to eat up the ones we do not want. I know that agricultural departments in some parts of the United States are already able to supply ladybirds, or ladybugs, and the eggs of praying mantids, so it may be worth inquiring from your local cooperative extension service to see what is available.

Pesticides

If you feel that the gentler methods outlined here are insufficient to deal with your pest problem, and that you simply must use a pesticide, do try first those that contain a good proportion of pyrethrum. Make sure it is intended for garden—not household—use. Malathion is possibly the next least harmful, but keep in mind that in the close space of a balcony, the harmful fumes will not dissipate as quickly as in the open space of a garden. Also be careful to remember that you will be brushing against the flowers and leaves more often on a balcony, and that pesticides such as malathion should not be in contact with the skin. Also, if you do have culinary herbs growing among your plants, take care that pesticide does not get on their leaves.

CHAPTER TWENTY-ONE

Holiday Care

One of the biggest problems facing all gardeners, whether their gardens are large or just little balcony squares, is what to do with the plants during times when they go away. There are several solutions, the best by far of course being the helpful neighbor, or the once-a-week cleaner who can often be induced to do a watering-instead-of-cleaning stint perhaps twice a week, or more if necessary. However, if you are not fortunate enough to possess this kind of cooperation, then it will be necessary to review the most protected areas of your domain, whether indoors or outdoors, into which as many as possible of the plants can be crowded together. I say

Gloxinia and calladiums.

"crowded together" advisedly, because they will give one another much more protection and shade in this way and will dry out more slowly than they will standing alone in wind and sun.

Wicks

If your absence is not to be a long one, put a bucket of water at the center of a tight grouping of potted plants. Make sure the bucket is standing higher than pots. Have a series of wicks extending from the bucket, one to each pot. Narrow strips of fabric will serve as wicks. Experiment first with what you have on hand to check widths and porosity. Perhaps you have some thick, absorbent pieces of string. Try it all out beforehand so that you will know just how much water will be transported in this way.

Plastic Bag

It will not matter if you leave your plant saucers filled with water before you go (unless you will be away in freezing weather). The plants can then take up this water to tide them over the first few days. A layer of sphagnum moss on the soil surface will do much to retain moisture, as will any flat stones you can add. A piece of clear plastic fitted around the stem and secured to the sides of the pot will create quite a lot of humidity. You can use large plastic bags for this, with the sides cut open. Clear plastic dry cleaners' bags are very useful here. If you have a number of small plants, this plastic bag technique will serve well if you simply encase the entire pot in the bag and tie the top of the bag around the stem of your plant. Start making a collection of bags in the weeks before you are to go away.

Plastic Sheet

Plastic sheets are very useful too. If your bathroom receives good light you can place all your plants in the bathtub cover them completely with the sheet, taping it to the tub so that the air is almost excluded. They should remain moist for a long period if well watered first. Be sure to use light-weight sheeting (polythene), which can be bought in varying widths and weights. Should you use this plastic tent technique, care must be taken that the plants are gradually reintroduced to the outer air. Remember that they will emerge from an unnaturally humid atmosphere, and may even have made new shoots in this "forcing" temperature. It will be necessary to leave them indoors for a few days, and even for the first day or two to leave them in the plastic bag or tent with the top open to accustom them to normal conditions. Disaster could follow an immediate return to outdoor conditions of sun and wind. You could leave a number of ferns or moisture-loving plants standing in an half-inch or so of water in the bathtub (without plastic covering) if you only plan to be away for a few days, but roots will begin to rot if left for too long.

Self-Watering System

It is possible to install self-watering systems that automatically water your plants at a certain time each day. Some people use these all the time to avoid daily watering, but there can be problems as all plants do not require the same amount irrespective of weather conditions. But for a few weeks' absence they can be very useful, if somewhat expensive. A series of little plastic tubes runs from a series of larger pipes to the soil of each plant, but this will need to be well tested out before leaving.

Sphagnum Moss

If you can find enough deep planters or containers to hold each pot, these could be packed with sphagnum moss between pot and planter, well watered first. This will hold moisture for quite a time. The surface soil needs a good layer of the moss also. There are other moisture-holding media such as vermiculite, peatmoss and chopped plastic foam. Even wet sand can be used, but it dries out more quickly than the moss.

People

None of these measures are as satisfactory as having somebody come in to water. Give them precise instructions about not watering plants which are already moist, or that have water already in their saucers.

Another alternative is to look for firms that specialize in caring for plants. Failing these, try one of those that supply and maintain plants for hotels, apartment buildings and so on. In leaving your plants with such firms, they will at least have expert attention. Even your local nursery might rise to the occasion, especially if you are a regular client. In the large building where we live, we have a *quid pro quo* arrangement among neighbors in the matter of plant-minding, but those who have to mind *ours* inherit a formidable task!

Mail Order Sources

Abundant Life Seed Foundation
P.O. Box 772
Port Townsend, WA 98368
(206) 385-5660
Over 600 varieties of open-pollinated and heirloom seeds of flowers, vegetables, wildflowers, trees and shrubs. Free catalog.

Bluestone Perennials
7211 Middle Range Road
Madison, OH 44057
(800) 852-5243
Over 400 varieties of perennials, including chrysanthemums, sedums and ground covers. Free catalog.

Borbaleta Gardens
15980 Canby Avenue
Faribault, MN 55021
(507) 334-2807
A variety of lilies, daylilies and irises. Catalog $3.

W. Atlee Burpee & Co.
200 Park Avenue
Warminster, PA 18974
(800) 333-5808
Perennial and annual flower and vegetable seeds. Free catalog.

Canyon Creek Nursery
3527 Dry Creek Road
Oroville, CA 95965
(916) 533-2166
Uncommon perennial plants, including varieties of salvia. Catalog $2.

Carlson's Gardens
Box 305
South Salem, NY 10590
(914) 763-5958
Azalea and rhododendron plants. Catalog $3 for 2-year subscription.

Carroll Gardens
P.O. Box 310
Westminster, MD 21158
(800) 638-6334
Broad selection of rare and unusual plants, including perennials, herbs, roses, evergreens, trees and shrubs. Catalog $3.

Chamblee's Rose Nursery
10926 U.S. Highway 69N
Tyler, TX 75706
(800) 256-7673
Old Garden Roses, miniature roses. Call for order form.

The Cook's Garden
P.O. Box 535
Londonderry, VT 05148
(802) 824-3400
Vegetable and herb seeds, also flowering vines, flowers and bulbs. Catalog $1.

Dutch Gardens
P.O. Box 200
Adelphia, NJ 07710
(908) 780-2713
Bulbs, including dahlias, tulips, narcissi, hyacinths and irises. Free catalog.

Forestfarm
990 Tetherow
Williams, OR 97544
(503) 846-7269
Perennials, including rare wildlife plants. Catalog $3.

Greer Gardens
1280 Goodpasture Island Road
Eugene, OR 97401
(800) 548-0111
Magnolias, azaleas, rhododendrons and perennials. Catalog $3.

Gurney's Seed and Nursery
110 Capital Street
Yankton, South Dakota 57079
(605) 665-1671
Flower and vegetable seeds. Free catalog.

**Henry Field's Seed and
Nursery Company**
415 North Burnett
Shenandoah, IA 51602
(605) 665-9391
Vegetable and fruit seeds, perennial plants
and seeds, bulbs, roses, fruit and nut trees and
berry plants. Free catalog.

Huff's Gardens
710 Juniatta Street
Burlington, KS 66839
(800) 279-4675
Chrysanthemums. Catalog $1.

J. E. Miller Nurseries, Inc.
5060 West Lake Road
Canandaigua, NY 14424
(800) 836-9630
Fruit, nut, flowering and shade trees, berry
plants, roses, ground covers and ornamental
grasses.

Jackson & Perkins
P.O. Box 1028
Medford, OR 97501
(800) 872-7673
Roses, bulbs and perennials. Free catalog.

Johnny's Selected Seeds
310 Foss Hill Road
Albion, ME 04910
(207) 437-4357
Vegetable, flower and herb seeds. Free catalog.

Klehm Nursery
4210 North Duncan Road
Champaign, IL 61821
(800) 533-3715
Peonies, tree peonies, hostas, daylilies, irises
and companion perennials.

Lofts Seed, Inc.
P.O. Box 146
Bound Brook, NJ 08805
(800) 526-3890
Turf and wildflower seeds.

Mellinger's
2310 West South Range Road
North Lima, OH 44452
(800) 321-7444
Perennials, wildflowers, bulbs, tropicals,
shrubs, ornamental grasses, berries, vines,
ground covers; shade, fruit and ornamental
trees. Free catalog.

The Mini-Rose Garden
P.O. Box 203
Cross Hill, SC 29332
(800) 996-4647
Miniature roses. Free catalog.

New Earth
3623 East Highway 44
Shepherdsville, KY 40165
(800) 462-5953
Vegetable, flower and herb seeds appropri-
ate for indoor or outdoor use grown hydro-
ponically or in soil. Also provides hydroponic
systems and supplies. Free catalog.

Nichols Garden Nursery
1190 North Pacific Highway
Albany, OR 97321
(503) 928-9280
Flower and vegetable seeds, including
herbs and unusual vegetables. Free catalog.

Park Seed Co.
Cokesbury Road
Greenwood, SC 29647
(800) 845-3369
Seeds of perennials, annuals and vegetables.

Redwood City Seed Company
P.O. Box 361
Redwood City, CA 94064
(415) 325-7333
Specializing in endangered cultivated veg-
etable, herb and specialty plants.

Richters
357 Highway 47
Goodwood, Ontario, Canada L0C 1A0
(905) 640-6677
Seeds, perennials and herbs.

Seeds Bl'm
HC 33 Idaho City Stage
Boise, ID 83706
(208) 342-0858

Specializing in heirloom seeds of vegetables, herbs and flowers. Catalog $3.

Shepherd's Garden Seeds
30 Irene Street
Torrington, CT 06793
(203) 482-3638
Varieties of vegetable and herb seeds bred for flavor. Free catalog.

Siskiyou Rare Plant Nursery
2825 Cummings Road
Medford, OR 97501
(503) 772-6846
Specializing in alpine and other dwarf hardy plants for the woodland and rock garden. Catalog $2.

Smith and Hawken
2 Arbor Lane, Box 6900
Florence, KY 41022
(800) 776-3336
Fruits, vegetables, vines and flowers. Free catalog.

Southern Exposure Seed Exchange
P.O. Box 170
Earlysville, VA 22936
(804) 973-4703
Specializing in heirloom varieties of vegetable seeds.

Spring Hill Nurseries
6523 North Galena Road
Peoria, IL 61656
(800) 582-8527
Flowers, including predesigned landscaping collections. Perennials, roses, ornamental trees, ground cover and hedges. Catalog $2.50.

Stokes Seeds, Inc.
Box 548
Buffalo, NY 14240
(800) 263-7233
Also in Canada:
Box 10
St. Catharines, Ontario, Canada L2R 6R6
Extensive variety of vegetable and flower seeds. Free catalog.

Teas
P.O. Box 1603
Bellaire, TX 77402

(800) 446-7723
Orchids, hibiscus, bark, cork, fertilizer, orchid and African violet supplies. Catalog $2.

Thompson & Morgan
P.O. Box 1308
Jackson, NJ 08527
(800) 274-7333
Annuals, fragrant flowers, climbers, bonsai, perennials, bulbs and vegetables. Free catalog.

Otis Twilley Seed Co.
P.O. Box 65
Trevose, PA 19053
(800) 622-7333
Vegetable and garden flower seed. Free catalog.

Van Bourgondien Bros.
P.O. Box 1000
Babylon, NY 11702
(800) 622-9997
Bulbs, perennials, clematis and lilies. Free catalog.

Vesey's Seeds, Ltd.
P.O. Box 9000
Calais, ME 04619
(800) 363-7333
Also in Canada:
Vesey's Seeds Ltd.
York, Prince Edward Island, Canada C0A 1P0
(902) 368-7333
Flower and vegetable seeds.

Wayside Gardens
1 Garden Lane
Hodges, SC 29695
(800) 845-1124
Wide selection of roses, shrubs, perennials, ornamental trees, vines and climbers and ground cover. Free catalog.

White Flower Farm
Litchfield, CT 06759
(203) 496-1661
Wide range of annuals, perennials and bulbs. Free catalog.

Wildseed Farms, Inc.
P.O. Box 308
Eagle Lake, TX 77434
(800) 848-0078
Specializing in wildflower seed. Catalog $2.

Index

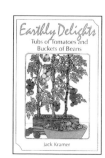